MW01089472

Rice University
Houston, Texas

Written by Julia Schwent

Edited by Adam Burns and Kimberly Moore

*Additional contributions by Omid Gohari,
Christina Koshzow, Christopher Mason, Joey Rahimi,
and Luke Skurman*

ISBN # 1-4274-0120-9
ISSN # 1551-9996
© Copyright 2006 College Prowler
All Rights Reserved
Printed in the U.S.A.
www.collegeprowler.com

Last updated on 2/23/06

Special Thanks To: Babs Carryer, Andy Hannah, LaunchCyte, Tim O'Brien, Bob Sehlinger, Thomas Emerson, Andrew Skurman, Barbara Skurman, Bert Mann, Dave Lehman, Daniel Fayock, Chris Babyak, The Donald H. Jones Center for Entrepreneurship, Terry Slease, Jerry McGinnis, Bill Ecenberger, Idie McGinty, Kyle Russell, Jacque Zaremba, Larry Winderbaum, Roland Allen, Jon Reider, Team Evankovich, Lauren Varacalli, Abu Noaman, Mark Exler, Daniel Steinmeyer, Jared Cohon, Gabriela Oates, David Koegler, and Glen Meakem.

Bounce-Back Team: Lucas Ogden-Davis, Courtney Dow, and Mark Pond.

College Prowler®
5001 Baum Blvd.
Suite 750
Pittsburgh, PA 15213

Phone: 1-800-290-2682
Fax: 1-800-772-4972
E-Mail: info@collegeprowler.com
Web Site: www.collegeprowler.com

How this all started...

When I was trying to find the perfect college, I used every resource that was available to me. I went online to visit school websites; I talked with my high school guidance counselor; I read book after book; I hired a private counselor. Sure, this was all very helpful, but nothing really told me what life was like at the schools I cared about. These sources weren't giving me enough information to be totally confident in my decision.

In all my research, there were only two ways to get the information I wanted.

The first was to physically visit the campuses and see if things were really how the brochures described them, but this was quite expensive and not always feasible. The second involved a missing ingredient: the students. Actually talking to a few students at those schools gave me a taste of the information that I needed so badly. The problem was that I wanted more but didn't have access to enough people.

In the end, I weighed my options and decided on a school that felt right and had a great academic reputation, but truth be told, the choice was still very much a crapshoot. I had done as much research as any other student, but was I 100 percent positive that I had picked the school of my dreams?

Absolutely not.

My dream in creating *College Prowler* was to build a resource that people can use with confidence. My own college search experience taught me the importance of gaining true insider insight; that's why the majority of this guide is composed of quotes from actual students. After all, shouldn't you hear about a school from the people who know it best?

I hope you enjoy reading this book as much as I've enjoyed putting it together. Tell me what you think when you get a chance. I'd love to hear your college selection stories.

Luke Skurman
CEO and Co-Founder
lukeskurman@collegeprowler.com

Welcome to College Prowler®

During the writing of College Prowler's guidebooks, we felt it was critical that the information within was unbiased, and that the guides were unaffiliated with any college or university. We think it's important that our readers get honest information and a realistic impression of the student opinions on any campus—that's why if any aspect of a particular school is terrible, we (unlike a campus brochure) intend to publish that fact. While we do keep an eye out for the occasional extremist—the cheerleader or the cynic—we take pride in letting the students tell it like it is. We strive to create a book that's as representative as possible of each particular campus. Our books cover both the good and the bad, and whether the survey responses point to recurring trends or a variation in opinion, these sentiments are directly and proportionally expressed through our guides.

College Prowler guidebooks are in the hands of students throughout the entire process of their creation. Because you can't make student-written guides without the students, we have students at each campus who help write, randomly survey their peers, edit, layout, and perform accuracy checks on every book that we publish. From the very beginning, student writers gather the most up-to-date stats, facts, and inside information on their colleges. They fill each section with student quotes and summarize the findings in editorial reviews. In addition, each school receives a collection of letter grades (A through F) that reflect student opinion and help to represent contentment, prominence, or satisfaction for each of our 20 specific categories. Just as in grade school, the higher the mark the more content, more prominent, or more satisfied the students are with the particular category.

Once a book is written, additional students serve as editors and check for accuracy even more extensively. Our bounce-back team—a group of randomly selected students who have no involvement with the project—are asked to read over the material in order to help ensure that the book accurately expresses every aspect of the university and its students. This same process is applied to the 200-plus schools College Prowler currently covers. Each book is the result of endless student contributions, hundreds of pages of research and writing, and countless hours of hard work. All of this has led to the creation of a student information network that stretches across the nation to every school that we cover. It's no easy accomplishment, but it's the reason that our guides are such a great resource.

When reading our books and looking at our grades, keep in mind that every college is different and that the students who make up each school are not uniform—as a result, it is important to assess schools on a case-by-case basis. Because it's impossible to summarize an entire school with a single number or description, each book provides a dialogue, not a decision, that's made up of 20 different topics and hundreds of student quotes. In the end, we hope that this guide will serve as a valuable tool in your college selection process. Enjoy!

OMID GOHARI ◯ CHRISTINA KOSHZOW ◯ CHRIS MASON ◯ JOEY RAHIMI ◯ LUKE SKURMAN ◯
The College Prowler Team

Table of Contents

By the Numbers............................ **1**

Academics **4**

Local Atmosphere **11**

Safety & Security **19**

Computers................................ **24**

Facilities.................................... **29**

Campus Dining......................... **34**

Off-Campus Dining **41**

Campus Housing **50**

Off-Campus Housing................ **59**

Diversity.................................... **65**

Guys & Girls.............................. **71**

Athletics.................................... **78**

Nightlife.................................... **86**

Greek Life **98**

Drug Scene............................. **102**

Campus Strictness **107**

Parking.................................... **112**

Transportation **117**

Weather **124**

Report Card Summary **128**

Overall Experience **129**

The Inside Scoop.................... **134**

Finding a Job or Internship **148**

Alumni **152**

Student Organizations............ **154**

The Best & Worst.................... **156**

Visiting **158**

Words to Know........................ **164**

Introduction from the Author

My sister, a fellow Rice alum, tells the story of the time she was grocery shopping in our small hometown of Festus, Missouri, wearing a sweatshirt that read, "RICE." The teller looked up at the sweatshirt several times before saying, "Wheat."

My sister raised her eyebrows, "Excuse me?"

"What about barley or corn?" replied the girl, sarcastically. "How random is your shirt? What if I had a shirt that just said, 'OATS' in bold print?" My sister then explained that it was the name of a university. The girl looked skeptical, but finished ringing up the groceries.

Outside of Texas and the world of academia, many people have never heard of Rice University (or at least, they had never heard of Rice before the school baseball team won the College World Series in the Spring of 2003). People that are knowledgeable about prestigious universities, however, will be impressed, and the average response from a Texas native is, "Wow, you go to Rice? You must be smart!" This slogan has actually been made into bumper stickers that read, "I go to Rice. I must be smart," and are traditionally hung upside down on students' car bumpers.

Rice has more to offer than a quirky sense of humor, high academic rankings, and a stellar baseball team. Rice also offers an exciting social scene, unique traditions, amazing research opportunities, a scenic campus located in an urban setting, and a vibrant, diverse student population.

Rice legend states that the University charter forbids any campus sidewalks or marked paths. William Marsh Rice, our founder, wanted Rice students to forge their own paths, rather than following the roads set neatly before them. While the University sidesteps this mandate by using the term "service roads," the underlying intention remains. The Rice atmosphere is one that encourages self-exploration and self-government, where students are not afraid to try new things and step out of their comfort zones.

Make no mistake: as you make your college decision, you are choosing a home, a lifestyle, and a future. Where will you spend the next four years, and how will this decision shape the person you will become? Is Rice University the right place for you? This guidebook is a unique overview of Rice U—its strengths and weaknesses, through the words and opinions of actual students and alumni. I hope that, by reading this book, you will gain helpful insight into the reality of the Rice experience.

Julia Schwent, Author
Rice University

By the Numbers

General Information

Rice University
PO Box 1892
Houston, Texas
77005 (Mail: 77251-1892)

Control:
Private

Academic Calendar:
Semester

Religious Affiliation:
None

Web Site:
www.rice.edu

Main Phone:
(713) 348-0000

Admissions Phone:
(713) 348-7423

Student Body

**Full-Time
Undergraduates:**
3,025

**Part-Time
Undergraduates:**
110

**Total Male
Undergraduates:**
1,556

**Total Female
Undergraduates:**
1,469

Admissions

Overall Acceptance Rate:
22%

Early-Action Acceptance Rate:
28%

Early Decision Acceptance Rate:
30%

Regular Acceptance Rate:
17%

Total Applicants:
8,106

Total Acceptances:
1,802

Yield (% of admitted students who actually enroll):
39%

Early Decision Available?
Yes

Early Action Available?
Yes

Early Decision One Deadline:
November 1

Early Decision Two Deadline:
December 1 (Interim)

Early Decision One Notification:
December 15

Early Decision Two Notification:
February 10 (Interim)

Regular Decision Deadline:
January 10

Regular Decision Notification:
April 1

Must-Reply-By Date:
January 2 (Early)
May 1 (Interim, Regular)

Students Accepted from Waiting List:
514

Students Enrolled from Waiting List:
40

Transfer Applications Received:
491

Transfer Applications Accepted:
105

Transfer Students Enrolled:
63

Transfer Student Yield:
60%

Common Application Accepted?
Yes

Supplemental Forms?
Yes

Admissions E-Mail:
admissions@rice.edu

Admissions Web Site:
www.rice.edu/prospect

→

SAT I or ACT Required?
Either

**SAT I Range
(25th–75th Percentile):**
1330–1540

**SAT I Verbal Range
(25th–75th Percentile):**
660–760

**SAT I Math Range
(25th–75th Percentile):**
670–780

**SAT II Requirements for
all departments:**
Writing and two additional
tests selected by applicant

Retention Rate:
92%

**Top 10% of
High School Class:**
86%

Application Fee:
$50

Financial Information

Tuition:
$20,160

Room and Board:
$8,980

Books and Supplies:
$800

**Average Need-Based
Financial Aid Package
(including loans, work-study,
grants, and other sources):**
$19,565

**Students Who Applied for
Financial Aid:**
74%

**Students Who Received
Financial Aid:**
32%

**Financial Aid Forms
Deadline:**
November 1 (Early Decision)
February 1 (Interim, Regular)

Financial Aid Phone:
(713) 348-4958

Financial Aid E-mail:
fina@rice.edu

Financial Aid Web Site:
www.ruf.rice.edu/~fina

Academics

The Lowdown On...
Academics

Degrees Awarded:
Bachelor
Master
Doctorate

Most Popular Majors:
8% Economics
6% English
5% Biological Sciences
5% Engineering
5% Social Sciences

Undergraduate Schools:
The School of Architecture
The George R. Brown School of Engineering
The School of Humanities
The Shepard School of Music
The Wiess School of Natural Sciences
The School of Social Sciences

→

Graduation Rates:

Four-year: 76%

Five-year: 89%

Six-year: 91%

Full-Time Faculty:

511

Faculty with Terminal Degree:

96%

Student-to-Faculty Ratio:

5:1

Average Course Load:

15 units per quarter

Best Places to Study:

Fondren Library

Ley Student Center

Residential College libraries

Quad areas

Dorm rooms

Sample Academic Clubs:

Tau Beta Phi Honor Society

Society of Women Engineers

National Society of Black Engineers

Pre-Medical Society

Phi Lambda Upsilon

National Society of Collegiate Scholars

Math Club

Rice Undergraduate History Majors' Society

Computer Science Club

Association of Latin American Engineers and Scientists

Architecture Society of Rice

American Institute of Chemical Engineers

Special Degree Options

Accelerated interdisciplinary legal education with Columbia University of Law, Combined M.D., advanced research degree for research careers in medicine with Baylor College of Medicine

Did You Know?

Two Rice professors are Nobel Laureates. For a complete list of Faculty Distinctions, visit: *www.ruf.rice.edu/~instresr/ricestatistics*

For their first semester, freshmen are allowed to drop classes up until the very last day of the semester. All students have the option to take four classes pass/fail during their college careers (no more than one in a given semester). This allows students to complete **those nasty distribution requirements** while putting forth minimum effort and concentrating more on classes in their majors.

AP Test Score Requirements
Possible credit for scores of 4 or 5

IB Test Score Requirements
Possible credit for scores of 6 or 7

Students Speak Out On...
Academics

"I've gone to one professor's house for a BBQ, and my physics professor brings us donuts at every review session—and I'm just a freshman!"

"The professors at Rice are amazing. Almost every professor is incredibly receptive to questions and concerns. They are tough but willing to help you do well in any way possible. Most classes are interesting, and **there are so many choices** that you can always find something to take."

"Incredible. **They are inspiring, very qualified, and passionate about what they do**. They are also very friendly with students. Plus, the classes are virtually all small. This semester, the number of people in my classes was, on average, about 15, so you get lots of personal interaction."

"It's like any university—**you have your good ones and your bad ones**. In smaller classes, you can get to know your professors better than in the bigger ones. If you take the time to ask them questions, visit their office hours, and show genuine interest, your profs will open up to you."

"**Teachers are so nice and enthusiastic** about their subjects. They are also very open-minded; they are willing to listen to your thoughts both in and out of class."

Q "Awesome profs! They know you by name, care about what you did last night, and even know the last prank you pulled! **Classes are interesting**, and thanks to their small size, very interactive."

Q "Generally, I found my teachers to be supportive, interesting, concerned with me, and generous with their time and advice. Exceptions include teachers who were very talented and charismatic, but **too self-absorbed to be much help outside of the classroom**, and teachers who were just plain boring. In terms of classes, I think I had a great time with all of the classes that I picked myself—i.e., classes I wasn't required to take (either electives in my major or classes outside of my department), and liked about half of the classes required of me. The ones I enjoyed least were classes I had to take for distribution in departments that otherwise held little interest for me."

Q "**My professors are intelligent, inquisitive, and very demanding**. They want to know their subjects inside and out, and they enjoy sharing their wealth of knowledge with inquiring minds."

Q "I found my classes at Rice University to be very interesting. They tend to be quite challenging but highly engaging, as well. **Class sizes are much smaller than those at comparable universities**, which provides a great deal of personal attention and guarantees that you'll always be able to speak to your profs about anything."

Q "**The teachers are wonderful at Rice**. They are not out to get you, and they genuinely want to help the students learn the material. As a result, they are very approachable and friendly. All of them hold office hours and will make appointments to see you. Most often, all it takes is a few words after class."

Q "The classes tend to be **pretty interesting**, at least the ones that I've taken. Some of the core classes are obviously not as fun to attend as the electives you can choose to take. However, there is a lot of variety, and there's always something for everyone."

Q "The teachers are very amiable. It's hard to generalize because they're varied. But generally, they're nice people, easy to get in touch with, and willing to help if you have a problem. **I find most of my classes here interesting**. I'm an English major, so most of my classes are discussion-based, which I really enjoy."

Q "The teachers are excellent in their knowledge about the subject, but they give hard exams and are really strict about homework and assignments. Since my major was engineering, **I have had the most challenging teachers**."

Q "The professors that I have had, so far, vary. I have had **excellent instructors, and not so good instructors**. But overall, they are extremely understanding. For example, if you have a situation that keeps you from turning in some assignment, they are willing to give you an extension. And you can always get in touch with them through e-mail!"

Q "Professors are very approachable. If you make an effort, you can definitely make sure they know your name. Most profs are willing to help out whenever you have questions—either via e-mail, or if you stop in at their office hours. It was really helpful for me to be at such a small school when I needed to get recommendations for summer programs. I feel like my professors have gotten to know me well. **It's more difficult to hide or get lost at Rice because it is so small**."

Q "The teachers make it easy to do well here because they really go out of their way to make sure everyone understands what they need to understand, and they **encourage thinking outside of the box**, so that you get a well-rounded education on top of it all."

The College Prowler Take On...
Academics

Rice students admit that most departments have both strong and weak professors. However, according to most undergrads, the overall experience with Rice professors is incredibly positive. Students rave about the close personal relationships that they form with many of their professors. They are approachable, eager to connect with students, very knowledgeable in their fields, and make every effort to be accessible to their students. They not only meet with students before and after class or during their office hours, but many also frequently eat lunch at local restaurants and attend University functions (athletic events, plays, and even off-campus social functions).

In order to earn a Rice degree, you must complete a certain number of classes in different areas of study (social sciences, humanities, science and engineering). This allows students the opportunity to explore academic areas outside of their chosen major. For many students, elective courses are an exciting change from their major courses. Because these distribution requirements can also be very challenging, Rice allows students to take four classes (not specifically required for their degree) pass/fail. This encourages students to take courses in subjects they are not familiar with, as well as allowing them to put more effort into their major classes than their distribution classes. However, when you do have a choice about your courses or professors, there are many resources to help you avoid unwise decisions.

A-

The College Prowler® Grade on
Academics: A-

A high Academics grade generally indicates that Professors are knowledgeable, accessible, and genuinely interested in their students' welfare. Other determining factors include class size, how well professors communicate, and whether or not classes are engaging.

Local Atmosphere

The Lowdown On...
Local Atmosphere

Region:
South

City, State:
Houston, Texas

Setting:
Major city

**Distance
from Dallas:**
4 hours

**Distance from
New Orleans:**
6 hours

➜

Points of Interest:

Hermann Park

The Houston Zoo

The Museum Of Natural Science (and the Butterfly Museum)

Nasa's Space Center Houston Museum

The Children's Museum

The Bayou Place

The Civic Center

The Wortham Theater Center

The Alley Theater

The George R. Brown Convention Center

The Jesse H. Jones Hall For The Performing Arts

Astrodome

Six Flags Astroworld

Galveston Beach

The San Jacinto Battlefield In Pasadena

Closest Shopping Malls:

Rice Village

University Blvd.

Houston, TX 77005

Cross Street: Between Kirby Drive & Greenbriar Drive

(Closest Shopping Malls, continued)

The Galleria

5085 Westheimer Rd., Suite 4850

Houston, TX 77056

(713) 622-0663

Closest Movie Theaters:

AMC Studio 30

2949 Dunvale

Houston, TX 77063

(281) 319-4AMC

Edwards Grand Palace Stadium 24

3839 Weslayan Street

Houston, TX 77027

(713) 871-8880

Angelika Film Center & Cafè

510 Texas Avenue

Houston, TX 77002

(713) 225-5232

Major Sports Teams:

Rockets (basketball)

Astros (baseball)

Texans (football)

City Web sites

www.cityofhouston.gov

www.chron.com

www.houston-guide.com

http://houston.citysearch.com

Did You Know?

Five Fun Facts about Houston:

• Houston passed up L.A. to become the "**#1 Smoggiest City in the Nation**" in 2000, but L.A. has since reclaimed its title.

• The first word spoken from the moon on July 20, 1969 was "**Houston**."

• The Heisman trophy is named for **John William Heisman**, the first full-time coach and athletic director at Rice University.

• The average yearly rainfall in West Texas is **less than eight inches**, while in East Texas (including the Houston area), the average exceeds 56 inches.

• Houston is **the home of several offbeat attractions**, including the National Museum of Funeral History, the Art Car Museum, and the Beer Can House (a house decorated by resident John Milkovisch with approximately 39,000 aluminum beer cans).

Famous People From Houston:

Howard Hughes, George Foreman, Barbara Mandrell, Dennis and Randy Quaid, Kenny Rogers, Lance Alworth, Debbie Allen, A. J. Foyt, William Marsh Rice, Ima Hogg, Dusty Hill, Beyoncé Knowles, Dan Rather, Mary Lou Retton, Carl Lewis, Brent Spiner, Debbie Allen, Jennifer Garner, Hilary Duff, George Bush Sr., Roger Clemens, Eva Mendes, Jaclyn Smith, Shannon Elizabeth

Local Slang:

Gulf freeway – Highway I-45

H-Town – Refers to Houston itself

The Loop – Refers to 610 Highway, which makes a loop around a large portion of Houston, not to be confused with the Inner and Outer loops of Rice University

TC – Taco Cabana, a popular 24-hour Mexican fast food joint

"Houston is a huge city, but I find it a little boring. Fortunately, because Rice has such a strong and tight-knit campus life, you don't really have to go out to have fun."

"Houston is a big town with lots of stuff to do, but Rice is pretty isolated from Houston. **Theoretically, you could go a whole year without leaving campus** and still enjoy yourself. There are other universities in Houston, but since Rice is so isolated, you don't meet many people from them, unless you make an effort to do so. Something to stay away from would be wandering around Houston at night, on foot. There's lots of stuff to visit: Hermann park, the zoo, the Astros, the Texans (unless you're a diehard Cowboys fan, like myself), Hurricane Harbor, the art museum, the Museum of Natural Science, the opera, the symphony, the Alley Theater, lots of really good restaurants, neat little coffeehouses, tapioca places in Chinatown, and more. There's tons of neat stuff to do."

"The atmosphere in this town is okay. **Houston is a boring place**; I will tell you that right now. Life ends here after 10 p.m. The best places are Transco Tower (a fountain park), Minute Maid Field (Astros), Six Flags, Waterworld, and the Reliant Center."

"I just go out to eat on weekends, that's about it. Everything I need is on campus. **Houston has some rough spots**, but it has never been a problem. There are a few other schools in Houston, as well."

Q "Houston's a big, growing city. There's plenty to do, like going to sporting events, concerts, and restaurants. We're really close to downtown, the museum district, and the medical district. A big city also means a lot of traffic. **It'll take a while to get across town**, but there's really no need to go far unless you want to."

Q "The atmosphere, I would say, is pretty decent. It's a very fun place to live. **There's plenty to do—from clubbing, to partying, to museums, to visiting the zoo** and the tons of restaurants—not to mention that it becomes an adventure when you try to get around Houston, due to the construction!"

Q "**Houston is big**, and Rice is near the center. The campus and its surroundings do have a very suburban feel to them, though. There are other universities and stuff to do in the city, but you rarely really venture beyond the Rice 'hedges' anyway."

Q "Houston is a great city **if you know where to go**, which can take a while to figure out. It has a small but thriving alternative community for those interested in modern and/or independent music, art, film, and politics. The Westheimer/Montrose district is a great place to find thrift stores and quirky cafes. The Menil Collection, the contemporary arts museum, and the Rothko Chapel are three stunning examples of smallish art venues. For film, try the Aurora Picture Show in the Heights."

Q "If you're interested in contemporary classical music, there are occasional concerts at the Axiom theatre (another great place for new theatre and rock shows). For more traditional fare, you can get decent student tickets to the Houston symphony and the **Houston Grand Opera**."

Q "Honestly, I am not a big fan of Houston, mostly because it's such a large city and I am more comfortable in more of a natural environment. But **I certainly have to admit that it does offer a lot to do and see**, with great museums and fantastic restaurants. And the good news is that if you don't like big cities very much either, the atmosphere on the Rice campus is entirely different. Total seclusion from the urban jungle can be found 'inside the hedges,' if you so desire."

Q "Houston is a huge metropolis. There are plenty of things to do in such a large city. However, I do not think that I have fully (or even remotely) taken advantage of what a city as large and diverse as Houston has to offer. Fortunately, Rice is also surrounded by some of Houston's greatest attractions: Hermann Park, a zoo, the Museum District, the Rice Village, and more. **Within a 15-minute walk, there are all sorts of interesting things to do**. If only I would get off my lazy butt and do them!"

Q "To be honest, I think that Houston is less than ideal. It's polluted, ugly, has sprawling strip malls, a less than perfect crime record, terrible weather, and virtually no public transportation. However, there are positive sides to living here. Rice is in what I consider to be the best neighborhood in the city. It's got the Rice Village, the Houston Medical Center (with over a dozen internationally-renowned hospitals), the Museum District, and several ritzy residential neighborhoods surrounding it. The food in Houston is fantastic, with a very cosmopolitan restaurant culture, and **the nightlife is pretty good** as well. There are other universities in the city, but Rice is pretty set apart and in its own little world. Rice students rarely go 'beyond the hedges' because everything we need is right here on campus."

"Just keep in mind that Houston is a very large city and **appropriate caution should be taken after dark**. Don't run alone on the outer loop at night, and don't walk anywhere alone when it's late out—even if you live two blocks from campus."

"**Houston's a city that grows on you**. Rice can be an island in the middle of the city—there's enough to do on campus that you never have to leave. But if you get out and look for stuff to do, there's plenty to be found."

The College Prowler Take On...
Local Atmosphere

Houston is the fourth largest city in the United States, and the urban sprawl, heavy traffic, and air pollution can be very intimidating at first. However, there are amazing advantages to living in a large city. Many Rice students acknowledge that the social life on campus is enough to keep students busy without needing to look beyond the Rice hedges for entertainment. However, outside of the Rice bubble, there is a world of diverse cultural and social opportunities to explore. Be sure to make time to experience the plethora of restaurants, museums, theaters, clubs, bars, sports teams, concerts, and everything else that Houston has to offer. While there are definitely areas of town that should be avoided late at night or when you are alone, students say that you only need to use common sense and exercise caution to guarantee your safety.

Do not compare Houston to New York, L.A., or Chicago. However, Houston does have something to offer for everyone. Overall, it is a fairly happening place for a young person to live. Go off the beaten path of typical Rice hangouts, and discover your own. If nothing else, you can keep things interesting by dining at a different restaurant every time you go out, and you probably won't run out of options before you graduate!

B+

The College Prowler® Grade on

A high Local Atmosphere grade indicates that the area surrounding campus is safe and scenic. Other factors include nearby attractions, proximity to other schools, and the town's attitude toward students.

Safety & Security

The Lowdown On...
Safety & Security

Number of Rice Police:
13, and 4 security personnel

Rice Police Phone:
(713) 348-6000

Safety Services:
Escort/van service
Emergency phones
(RAD) Rape Agression Defense classes
Campus Watch

Health Services:
Basic medical services
Immunizations
STD screening
Pregnancy tests
Birth control
Counseling and psychological services

Health Center Office Hours:
Monday–Friday 8:30 a.m.–5 p.m., Closed for lunch 12:30 p.m.–1 p.m.

Did You Know?

Rice has its own police department, known as RUPD. **They are not rent-a-cops**, but an actual Houston police department, with officers who are hand-picked to work here. Each residential college has an officer assigned specifically to their college. The officers host an annual study break, known as "Cookies and Cops," at each residential college to discuss campus safety and security with students.

Students Speak Out On...
Safety & Security

{ **"Considering that Houston is such a big city, I feel very safe on the Rice campus. The campus police are amazing, and their constant presence around campus makes me feel really secure."**

"I have always felt safe on campus. **Rice students are trustworthy**, and I don't worry too much about people who don't belong on-campus being on campus. Houston is a large city with a crime problem, but Rice seems to be left out of that mess."

"**I feel pretty safe on campus**. All the entrances except for one are locked after midnight, which can be a pain, but it helps to prevent random people being on campus late at night. The campus police are always around, and they're generally good about staying in touch with the students."

"The security officers are helpful, but I would advise you not to go out at night alone, and always be around friends because it is in the downtown area. Since it's an open university, people can get in and out easily. So yes, the security is good, but nothing is perfect. **I myself have never faced any kind of problems**; neither has anyone I know."

"Security is pretty good here. There's a campus escort if you're uncomfortable and it's late. **It's in a nice part of Houston, even though it is downtown**, so it's not scary around campus."

💬 "On campus is pretty safe. **Once you leave the hedges, you are in Houston, which can be unsafe**—like any city. You just have to be aware of your surroundings. I feel completely safe walking back from the library to my college at 2 a.m. all by myself."

💬 "**I always felt safe walking around on campus whatever the hour**, but a rash of on-campus crime the last few months has made me retrospectively more wary. However, the campus police are around all the time, there are lots of blue-light phones, and the small campus means you're always near some building or another. So, in general, I'd say the campus is very safe."

💬 "Security is wonderful! The emergency medical technicians (EMTs) have an average response time of something like one minute and 45 seconds, which is faster than the local ambulance and fire department. **There are emergency blue telephones scattered across campus**, so that you can call for help anywhere on campus at any given time."

💬 "There was never any moment during my four years at Rice when I felt unsafe in any way. **Crime is virtually non-existent here**. The campus police are excellent, and they do a very good job of keeping things secure without making things difficult for the students."

💬 "I've never felt unsafe or endangered in all my time at Rice. There are 27 full-time police officers who are licensed by the state of Texas to protect us, and they have all of the authority of normal police officers. There are blue-light phones that are situated such that, no matter where you are on campus, you will be able to see one and get to it in a reasonable amount of time in case of an emergency, and police response is almost immediate. **Having these systems in place makes Rice safe**. This, however, does not mean that you can let your guard down. The key to staying safe, especially since we are an open campus in the middle of the fourth largest city in the country, is to stay alert and aware."

The College Prowler Take On...
Safety & Security

Although situated in the heart of a huge city, the Rice campus, for the most part, feels like it's sealed by an invisible, protective forcefield. Most Rice students feel exceptionally safe and secure on campus. The Rice University Police Department goes to great lengths to keep the campus secure and build a positive relationship with the student body. While many students complain about the severity of parking ticket enforcement, the overall consensus is that the RUPD does the best they can to ensure the safety and comfort of college student on campus. In other words, they are not out to bust crazy college kids and drain their meager bank accounts; they are here to protect and serve the student body and make sure a productive learning environment is not disturbed by unwanted outsiders.

The safety services (blue-light phones, escorts, dorm alarms) are very effective and helpful. While there have been a few isolated incidents of theft or trespassing in the last few years, most students agree that they have never felt unsafe at Rice, and many students feel comfortable enough with campus security to leave their rooms unlocked.

A

The College Prowler® Grade on

Safety & Security: A

A high grade in Safety & Security means that students generally feel safe, campus police are visible, blue light phones and escort services are readily available, and safety precautions are not overly necessary.

Computers

The Lowdown On...
Computers

High-Speed Network?
Yes

Wireless Network?
Yes

Number of Labs:
27

Number of Computers:
523

Charge to Print?
Yes

Operating Systems:
Windows, Mac, UNIX

Free Software:
McAfee Total Defense Suite, F-Secure SSH, X-Win32, SSH Communications Security's SSH

24-Hour Labs:
All residential college labs, Mud, Ryon, Fondren. Most labs are open 24 hours if you have access to the building.

Students Speak Out On...
Computers

{ **"The network is good, and the labs are rarely crowded, but owning a computer is a plus."**

Q "I'd definitely suggest bringing your own computer. The computers in the library fill up quite fast at peak times. There are several other labs that are probably less busy, so **I'm sure you could get away with not having a computer of your own**, but I wouldn't suggest it."

Q "The network is fast, and going home and using dial-up is always a drag for me. **There are plenty of computer labs on campus**. They are probably rather underutilized because so many people have their own computers. In addition, the Unix computers found across campus are not as user-friendly for the uneducated Unix user as the computer-gurus like to think. This might also discourage people from using the computer labs as much as they might otherwise use them. One doesn't need a personal computer, per se, but I only know one person on campus that doesn't have one."

Q "The computer network at Rice is excellent. While bringing your own computer and printer is recommended, there are plenty of computers available both in the residential dorms and scattered throughout the campus for student use. **Most of the labs are not overly crowded**, though they can get congested during heavy projects and during finals and midterms."

Q "**Have a computer in your dorm room**. You don't want to always be on your roommate's, and you probably won't want them always on yours."

Q "Broadband kicks [butt]! **I come from a 56k modem home, and the Internet connection here is much better** for downloading stuff (while being sure to comply with all copyright laws, of course). The residential colleges all have computer labs of varying quality, but it's much more convenient to bring your own computer."

Q "**People will say you don't need your own computer**, but it is certainly recommended. I think if you can get one, it would be more to your advantage. Because nearly everyone at Rice has a computer, though, it is not a problem to use the ones on campus. I tend to use the ones in the library to write papers just because it helps me focus more."

Q "I can't imagine not having a computer because I used it all the time for my major. **I would say that you can always find a computer to use** if you need one and can't bring one of your own. The computer labs are also very nice. Aside from Mudd Lab, which is the main one on campus, there are lots of little ones spread around—in the architecture building and the physics hall, for example."

Q "**The Ethernet computer network at Rice is highly advanced and very fast**. There are numerous labs scattered around campus with plenty of computers (both Macs and PCs), but many students choose to bring their own computer and printer for convenience and/or entertainment."

Q "**I would suggest bringing your own computer**. It is very useful, but it is not necessary. Computer labs are not always crowded. I use the computer lab half the time, and my own computer the other half of the time."

Q "**Computers are not necessary at Rice** because there are computer labs located in all of the departments, major buildings, labs, colleges, and in the library. However, I recommend bringing a computer just for ease of use."

Q "I'd bring a computer. Laptop vs. desktop, PC vs. Mac—it really doesn't matter. It's entirely one's preference because all systems are supported here. **There is a main computing lab on campus that's open to all students 24 hours a day** during the week, and until late on the weekends. It's full of PC, Mac, and Unix labs, as well as all of the printing, scanning and burning equipment. There is also an Information Technology system in place with technicians who can help students with any problems they might have. The network is really nice at Rice, as well. We share a T3 line with the University of Houston and the Houston Med Center, so every room on campus has really fast Ethernet ports available for student use (one for each person in the room)."

The College Prowler Take On...
Computers

Students admit that you can get by without your own computer here. Rice has enough labs to go around, and the hours and locations are convenient to all. The labs are popular places to work, as they offer fewer distractions than the residential halls. Overcrowding is rarely a problem, and both Macs and PCs are available.

However, for the sake of convenience, a personal laptop or desktop is highly recommended. High-speed Ethernet is available and free to all students, both within the dorms and across campus, and computers are probably the most widely used form of communication within the Rice community. Instant Messages and e-mails are constantly flying back and forth (sometimes even between roommates—so sad). A Rice student is more likely to IM a person two rooms down the hall to ask a question than to actually trot down the hall and do it in person.

The College Prowler® Grade on

A high grade in Computers designates that computer labs are available, the computer network is easily accessible, and the campus' computing technology is up to date.

Facilities

The Lowdown On...
Facilities

Student Center:
Ley Student Center

Campus Size:
300 acres

Athletic Center:
Autry Court

Popular Places to Chill:
Fondren Library
Residential College Commons and Quad areas
The Student Center
The Engineering Quad

Libraries:
Fondren Library

What Is There to Do on Campus?

On campus, you can go swimming, pump some iron, or practice other sports at Autry Court. Students can also get a coffee, smoothie, beer, or sub sandwich at the student center, take in an independent film or use the photo labs in the Media Center, see an exhibition of a contemporary artist at the Rice Gallery in Sewell Hall, or go see a play or musical in Hamman Hall or any of the nine residential colleges.

Movie Theater on Campus?

The Media Center

Bar on Campus?

Yes, Valhalla or Willy's Pub

Coffeehouse on Campus?

Yes, RMC/ Ley Student Center

Bowling on Campus?

No

Favorite Things to Do

Pub night on Thursdays at Willy's Pub is very popular with most underclassmen, although seniors and grad students prefer to go to the calmer Valhalla pub (also on campus). The Coffeehouse in the student center does good business late into the night (closes at 12 a.m.), and they sometimes host open-mic nights, poetry slams, and small concerts. The Undergrounds, located in the basement of Lovett College, is a cozy candlelit venue for student musicians and performers, and the coffee and hot chocolate are free (donations encouraged). Shepard Music Hall is a source of frequent, free, and amazing concerts and operas. Rice Dance Theater, the Rice Philharmonics (an a capella group) and Spontaneous Combustion (an improv comedy group) all perform frequently in various spaces on campus, often to large crowds. The Rice Players and the residential colleges put on amazing theatrical productions, many of which are student produced and directed. IM sports are huge, and some varsity sports are popular as well, with free admission to students.

Students Speak Out On...

Facilities

"The facilities are first rate, among the best in the country. However, the athletic facilities are only average. The University's main emphasis is on academics, and you'll notice it."

"It's definitely nice, but because Rice is small, the student center facilities are not wonderful. The **convenience store is really limited in its selection**."

"**The gym is swank**, outfitted with personal TV screens for every cardio machine and a huge weight room. It gets very crowded, and during busy times you may not get the machine you want, but it's a great facility."

"The facilities are good. Autry Court is where people work out—apparently, it has many new improvements. **Rice Coffeehouse is super good**."

"In the past few years, Rice has built and renovated a number of buildings. Consequently, **there are several amazing facilities around campus**. However, there are other buildings that appear to never have been touched since their opening, decades ago."

"**The campus facilities are, for the most part, very good**. A few have been around for a very long time and are being renovated, but there are quite a number of new buildings that are very well designed and well furnished."

"The gym is somewhat small, but since Rice has a small

student body, it's never too incredibly crowded, and the equipment is in good shape. **The college computer labs are of varying quality**, but the labs in the academic buildings are pretty nice, though you can't get into those late at night."

Q "The facilities are awesome. **The campus is quite beautiful**, and many of the buildings are richly furnished, adorned, and equipped for the 21st-century student."

Q "The gym is decent, although it's not as good as some schools I've visited. **The student center is pretty basic, nothing spectacular**."

Q "Facilities are pretty good. The gym has been remodeled in the last couple years, and it has a lot of great options. Many students go there to work out in groups and individually. **The recreation center also offers many different fitness programs** and neat courses to students, faculty, staff, and alumni. However, even though it has undergone a lot of great changes, the gym is still a little outdated, and I think they are talking about redoing it. The student center is a great place to hang out, and many off-campus residents spend quite a lot of time there. Many of the main student organizations have offices in the student center, as well as most student services such as Career Services, Academic Advising, and the Study Abroad Office."

Q "In the student center, there are also **many different lounges and conference rooms available** for Rice community use, as well as the campus bookstore. There's also a Kinko's, a convenience store, a Subway, a student-run Coffeehouse, a cafeteria, an undergraduate student pub, and a Smoothie King."

The College Prowler Take On...
Facilities

Students feel lukewarm about Rice facilities. Over the last couple years, there has always been one construction project or another going on to improve facilities. The noise pollution and ugly construction equipment can be a nuisance, but the improvements made to the Rice gym, the student center, and several academic and residential buildings, with the addition of the food serveries, new college commons, and other new buildings (Martel College, the new Wiess College, and the Jones Graduate School of Business, for example) seem to be worth the trouble.

Fortunately, all students can enjoy the new and old food options at the student center, and afterward attempt to burn off these options at the Rice gym. The recent addition of small television screens to each treadmill, elliptical machine, and exercise bike has been a popular one. However, the TVs are not always in the best of shape, and a few have problems with static, or are unable to receive certain channels. The Rice Media center offers a photo lab, which is open to anyone in the Rice or Houston community. However, in order to use the lab, you must either take a photography class or demonstrate that you have previous training. The movie theater located in the same building is small and cozy, and shows an excellent variety of exotic movies (usually foreign or independent films).

The College Prowler® Grade on
Facilities: B

A high Facilities grade indicates that the campus is aesthetically pleasing and well maintained, facilities are state-of-the-art, and libraries are exceptional. Other determining factors include the quality of both athletic and student centers and an abundance of things to do on campus.

Campus Dining

The Lowdown On...
Campus Dining

Freshman Meal Plan Requirement?

Yes

Meal Plan Average Cost:

$1,540 per semester (on campus)

$620 per semester (off campus)

Places to Grab a Bite with Your Meal Plan:

The Coffeehouse

Location: The Student Center

Food: Coffee/espresso drinks, tea, baked goods

Favorite Dish: Hot chai or Snickerdoodles

Hours: Monday–Thursday 8 a.m.–12 a.m., Friday 8 a.m.–5 p.m., Sunday 8 p.m.–12 a.m.

→

The Pub

Location: The Student Center

Food: Smoothies, sandwiches, pizza, beer

Favorite Dish: The sub sandwiches are yummy!

Hours: Monday 11 a.m.–1 a.m., Tuesday–Thursday 11 a.m.–2 p.m., Friday 11 a.m.–5 p.m.

Residential College Serveries

Location: Residential Colleges

Food: Buffet Style, grill, pizza, salad bar, vegetarian option, dessert

Favorite Dish: Lentil Stew, Wok stir–fry, omelets, desserts

Hours: Monday–Friday 7:30 a.m.–9:30 a.m., Continental 9:30 a.m.–11 a.m., 11:30 a.m.–1:30 p.m., 5:30 p.m.–7:30 p.m., Saturday–Sunday 11:30 a.m.–1:30 p.m., Sunday 5 p.m.–7 p.m.

Sammy's

Location: The Student Center

Food: Smoothie King, grill (sandwiches, pizza, burgers, fries), hot food, pre–packaged (salads, fruit, sushi, chips, cereal, cookies)

Favorite Dish: It's all pretty darn good!

Hours: Monday–Friday 11 a.m.–2 p.m.

Subway

Location: The Student Center

Food: Sandwiches, salads, cookies, chips

Favorite Dish: Carnitas sub, meatball sub, cookies

Hours: Monday–Wednesday, Friday 7:30 a.m.–11 p.m., Thursday 7:30 a.m.–1 a.m., Saturday 11:00 a.m.–11 p.m., Sunday 12 p.m.–11 p.m.

Off-Campus Places to Use Your Meal Plan:

None

24-Hour On-Campus Eating?

No

Student Favorites:

The Coffeehouse

Subway

Smoothie King

Did You Know?

Older students on campus will occasionally refer to food from the residential college serveries as CK, or "Central Kitchen." Until the completion of the two large campus serveries a few years ago, **all the food served at the colleges was prepared in one building**, the Central Kitchen, and then shipped to the individual colleges to be reheated. While the Central Kitchen system is no longer in use, the term has not yet vanished from the vocabulary of Rice undergrads.

Other Options

Cohen House, also called the Faculty Club, is a restaurant on campus with high-quality food and a nice sit-down atmosphere. However, it is primarily meant to serve faculty and staff, and students are permitted only upon invitation by a faculty or staff member.

Students Speak Out On...
Campus Dining

{

"The new serveries are great! There is a great selection, and the lines are short. There has been a huge improvement from when I entered."

Q "The food is okay, but I'm sure it is better than a lot of other places. **There is a big choice, and they're always trying to improve**. There's a Subway in the student center with long hours, and Sammy's is another good spot for lunch."

Q "**Food at Rice is now very respectable**. It has improved tremendously over the last couple of years, and is now actually very good. I'd say that it compares favorably with other first-rate schools."

Q "The food has improved significantly over the last few years, and at this point, it's safe to say you'll be able to find something to eat every night no matter what your dining restrictions. However, it is cafeteria food, which is to say that at best, it's healthy, filling and inoffensive, but not particularly 'good.' There are exceptions (lentil stew and brownie pie are my favorites), and **you can always get a burger or pasta** every night if you don't mind a homogenous diet."

Q "**Food at Rice is really not that good**. It is cafeteria food, but they are changing the meal plan for next semester so that we will have access to the cafeteria for more than just a few hours during the day. The only restaurants on campus are Subway and Cohen House, but Cohen House is mostly for teachers."

Q "Food on campus is not half bad. The residential college system allows for there to be a number of small cafeterias that make the dining situation better. **At my residential college, we have family-style dinners every night** where we sit down, and freshmen wait on upperclassmen. It's a really fun tradition."

Q "Since the new serveries came in, food has improved 100 percent. Unfortunately, the Rice meal plan charges rather steep prices as a result of the improvements. **The salad bar is pretty great, and the desserts are good**. Personally, I love the omelets, which are made to order on Saturday and Sunday mornings for brunch. You can definitely find something to eat every day, but sometimes the menu begins to feel monotonous."

Q "The food at the new campus serveries has recently been rated as some of the best food at colleges around the country. **Professional chefs are given a great deal of room in which to work**, and new developments and refinements come along frequently."

Q "**Each residential college has its own commons** and either its own servery, or a servery shared with only a few colleges. You can eat at any college you want with your card. I think the food at the bigger serveries is good, but the meal plan is really expensive. Some of the smaller serveries have not-so-good food."

Q "With the new dorms recently opened, food is actually decent. We have the residential college system, and food is relatively good, especially compared to years ago. One thing, however, you will get sick of it! After eating different things, you will get sick of it regardless of how good it is. That's okay, though, because Houston has the most restaurants per capita, and it's super cheap to eat here. **There are plenty of places around Rice and in Houston to eat**."

Q "**Food on campus is kind of blah**; there are not a lot of options. The residential colleges are all getting these new serveries now that offer a lot more options, and the food is better because it is fresher—they don't have to ship it from one central location anymore."

Q "The food is edible. All things considered, it's pretty good. However, quality varies across campus. The best food is at the South College Servery. Chef Roger is in charge there, and the food is both tasty and interesting. The rest of the food across campus is alright. It varies from day to day how good it is, and after three years of eating it, the repetition gets tiresome. **Things are often overcooked after sitting out for a while**, and it's sometimes questionable if the meat is even really meat. But it is also possible to eat well. The salad bar is usually very good, and there are always vegetarian and health-conscious options available. The desserts are usually fantastic. And if all else fails, there is always Subway in the student center or plenty of great (and not too expensive) restaurants in the Village."

The College Prowler Take On...
Campus Dining

Compared to larger universities, the number of on-campus dining options at Rice is very limited. Aside from cafeteria options, the student center offers a Smoothie King, Subway, Coffee House, Willy's Pub, and Sammy's (upscale Cafeteria food). Lucky students might get an invite from Rice faculty to dine at Cohen House, but many students graduate without ever stepping inside.

Upperclassmen rave about the improvements that have been made in campus dining over the last several years. Subway and Smoothie King have both opened in recent years, and the addition of three college serveries (in the place of the old Central Kitchen system) has greatly increased the quality and variety of food offered at the residential colleges. The cost of the undergrad meal plan has steadily increased with the improvements, but students can choose from vegetarian options, a salad and fruit bar, sandwiches, pizza, grill food, soup, desert, baked goods, cereal, made-to-order omelets (only on weekends), or main dishes. The serveries will also occasionally offer a themed food night that provides extra options (Italian Night, Pacific Rim, Open-Wok-Make-Your-Own-Stir-Fry Night, and more). It is, after all, still cafeteria food, but most students have no problem finding something tolerable to eat, and many dishes actually turn out to be fairly tasty.

The College Prowler® Grade on
Campus Dining: B-

Our grade on Campus Dining addresses the quality of both school-owned dining halls and independent on campus restaurants as well as the price, availability, and variety of food available.

Off-Campus Dining

The Lowdown On...
Off-Campus Dining

Restaurant Prowler:
Popular Places to Eat!

Amazon Grill
Food: Central/South American

5140 Kirby, Houston

(713) 522-5888

Cool Features: Free plantain chips and salad, outdoor seating

Price: $5–$12 per person

Hours: Monday–Thursday 11 a.m.–10 p.m., Friday–Saturday 11 a.m.–11 p.m. Sunday 11a.m.–9 p.m.

Amy's Ice Cream
Food: Ice cream, coffee

3816 Farnham, Houston

(713) 526-2697

Cool Features: Smash Ins—you get to pick your toppings and watch the workers beat it into your ice cream with really big spoons

Price: $3–$5 per person

Hours: Sunday–Thursday 11:30 a.m.–12 a.m., Friday–Saturday 11:30 a.m.–1 a.m.

➜

Auntie Chang's Dumpling House

Food: Chinese

2621 S. Shepherd Dr., Ste. 290, Houston

(713) 524-8410

Price: $15–$10 per person

Hours: Monday–Thursday 11 a.m.–10 p.m., Friday 11 a.m.–10:30 p.m., Saturday 11:00 a.m.–10:30 p.m.

Biba's Greek Restaurant

Food: Greek

607 W Gray St., Houston

(713) 523-0425

Price: $8–$12 per person

Hours: Daily 24 hours

Buca di Beppo

Food: Italian

5192 Buffalo Speedway, Houston

(713) 665-2822

Cool Features: Fun atmosphere, family-style dining

Price: $15–$20 per person

Hours: Monday–Thursday 5 p.m.–10 p.m., Friday 5 p.m.–11 p.m., Saturday 4 p.m.–11 p.m., Sunday 12 p.m.–9 p.m.

Buffalo Wild Wings

Food: Wings

11803 Westheimer Rd., Houston

(281) 497-WING (9464)

Price: $8–$12 per person

Hours: Sunday–Monday 11 a.m.–12 p.m., Tuesday–Saturday 11 a.m.–2 a.m.

Chuy's Restaurant

Food: Tex–Mex

2706 Westheimer Rd., Houston

(713) 524-1700

Cool Features: Fun "frat-party" atmosphere, bar, creamy jalapeno dip

Price: $15–$25 per person

Hours: Sunday–Thursday 11 a.m.–11 p.m., Friday–Saturday 11 a.m.–12 a.m.

The Cheesecake Factory

5015 Westheimer Rd., Houston

(713) 840-0600

Cool Features: Over 200 menu items

Price: $15–$20 per person

Hours: Monday–Thursday 11 a.m.–11 a.m. Friday–Saturday 11 a.m.–12 p.m., Sunday 10 a.m.–10 p.m.

Dimassi's Middle Eastern Café

Food: Middle Eastern

2401 Times Blvd., Houston

(713) 526-5111

Cool Features: All-you-can-eat buffet

Price: $10–$15 per person

Hours: Daily 11 a.m.–9 p.m.

Freebirds World Burrito

Food: Huge burritos!

3745 Greenbriar St., Houston

(713) 524-0621

Cool Features: Outside seating

Price: $5–$12 per person

Hours: Sunday–Thursday 11 a.m.–9:30 p.m., Friday–Saturday 11 a.m.–10:30 p.m.

Fu's Garden

Food: Chinese

2539 University Blvd.

(713) 520-7422

Cool Features: Good lunch specials

Price: $6–$12 per person

Hours: Sunday–Thursday 11 a.m.–10 p.m., Friday–Saturday 12 p.m.–11 p.m.

Hobbit Hole Cafe

2243 Richmond Ave., (at Portsmouth), Houston

(713) 528-3418

Cool Features: *Lord of the Rings* artwork enlivens the walls

Price: $5–$10 per person

Hours: Monday–Thursday 11 a.m.–9:30 p.m., Friday 11 a.m.–10:30 p.m., Saturday 10:30 a.m.–10:30 p.m., Sunday 10:30 a.m.–9 p.m., Brunch (along with full menu) 10:30 a.m.–1:30 p.m.

House of Pies

Food: American diner, pies

3112 Kirby Dr., Houston

(713) 528-3816

Price: $5–$10 per person

Hours: Daily 24 hours

Istanbul Grill

Food: Turkish

Address: 5613 Morningside Dr., Houston

(713) 526-2800

Price: $5–$10 per person

Hours: Tuesday–Sunday 10 a.m.–10 p.m.

Jason's Deli

Food: Deli sandwiches, salads, soups, baked potatoes

2530 University Blvd., Rice Village

(713) 522-2660

Cool Features: Salad Bar, Free soft–serve ice cream

Price: $5–$10 per person

Hours: Monday–Thursday 8 a.m.–10 p.m., Friday– Saturday 8 a.m.–11 p.m., Sunday 8 a.m.–10 p.m.

Le Peep

Food: American

4702 Westheimer Rd., Houston

(713) 629-7337

Cool Features: Great withspecial requests

Price: $5–$10 per person

Hours: Weekdays 6:30 a.m.–2:30 p.m., Weekends 7 a.m.–2:30 p.m.

Mai's Restaurant

Food: Vietnamese

3403 Milam St., Houston

(713) 520-7684

Cool Features: Open super late, TVs, fish tank

Price: $5–$10 per person

Hours: Sunday–Thursday 10 a.m.–3 a.m., Friday– Saturday 10 a.m.–4 a.m.

Niko Niko's

Food: Greek

2520 Montrose, Houston

(713) 528-1308

Fax: (713) 529-9442

Price: $8–$15 per person

Hours: Sunday–Thursday 10 a.m.–9 p.m., Friday– Saturday 10 a.m.–11 p.m.

Nit Noi Thai

Food: Thai

2426 Bolsover St., Houston

(713) 524-8114

Price: $20–$25 per person

Hours: Monday–Friday 11 a.m.–3 p.m., Monday– Friday 5 p.m.–10 p.m., Saturday–Sunday 11 p.m.– 10 p.m.

Star Pizza

Food: Pizza

2111 Norfolk St., Houston

(713) 523-0800

Cool Features: Low–carb pizza

Price: $5–$10 per person

Hours: Monday–Thursday, Sunday 11a.m.–10:30 p.m., Friday–Saturday 11 a.m.– 12 a.m.

Taco Cabana
Food: Mexican Fast Food
3905 Kirby Drive, Houston
(713) 528-6933
Cool Features: Outdoor seating, really cheap tortillas and queso
Price: $1– $10 per person
Hours: Daily 24 hours

Teahouse
Food: Tapioca Pearl Tea (a.k.a. Bubble/Boba Tea)
2089 Westheimer Rd., Houston
(713) 526-6123
Cool Features: Board games to play while you drink
Price: $3–$5 per person
Hours: Sunday–Thursday 10 a.m.–10 p.m., Friday–Saturday 10 a.m.–12 a.m.

Closest Grocery Stores:
Fiesta Mart
12355 Main Street
(713) 551-7575

Kroger Food Stores - Southwest
5150 Buffalo Speedway
(713) 661-8305

Fun Facts:
The Rice Student Association, (SA) distributes Silver Saver Cards, which entitle students to discounts at local restaurants.

Student Favorites
House of Pies, Teahouse, Mai's Vietnamese, Biba's Greek, Fu's Garden

Best Pizza:
Star Pizza

Best Breakfast:
Le Peep Restaurant

Best Healthy:
Hobbit Café

Best Wings:
Buffalo Wild Wings

Best Place to Take Your Parents:
The Cheesecake Factory

Other Places to Check Out:
Two Rows, Lai Lai's, Thai Spice, Miss Saigon, Ruggles, La Madeline, Kin's, Quiznos, Masraff;s, America's, Texadelphia, Goode Company Texas Seafood, 29 Diner, Houston's, Brasil, Barnaby's, Paulie's, Chapultipec, Yan Sushi, Bubba's, IHOP

Students Speak Out On...

Off-Campus Dining

"Oh, Houston restaurants are amazing. I think we have the most restaurants per capita in the nation, and there are all sorts of awesome foods nearby."

Q "There are tons of great places all around Rice, especially in the Rice Village—all cuisines, price ranges, and atmospheres, from buffalo wings, to tapas, to pizza, to Chinese, to Cuban. There's **just anything you could possibly want**. Chinatown is close too, and there are tons of great places there."

Q "There are a lot of really good restaurants in Houston, but you need to drive to them because they are all spread out. The Rice Village is nice, but it's quite a walk across the parking lot to get there, so **most meals you eat will be on campus**."

Q "You can eat at the Istanbul Grill, a Greek restaurant, a burrito joint, Jason's Deli, burger places, Cuban places, Mexican places, a French bakery, a smoothie place, lots of Thai places, Two Rows—**all located in Rice Village, within walking distance of campus**."

Q "I mainly go to the ones that are open 24-hours. Taco Cabana is a cheap Mexican place with good tortillas and decent queso. The House of Pies has great pie and good breakfast food, too. **Rice is right in the middle of Houston**, so there are hundreds of restaurants around. Just about anything you want, you can find."

Q "Houston is a great city, culturally. **You want it, Houston's got it**. It might be a drive away, but it's around. Fortunately, Rice is conveniently located next to the Rice Village (full of great restaurants) and near downtown (also full of good restaurants). Some favorites: Lai Lai's in China Town, Thai Spice (the village), and Miss Saigon (Vietnamese food)."

Q "I love Houston restaurants. I've been spoiled rotten living here, and I've discovered my absolute passion for Asian food (the Asian food in Houston is fabulous). I go home to my small town during the summers and I'm lost. Suddenly the town's Chinese buffet seems so disappointing. I spend three months every year just **counting the days until I can come back** to school and go out for some Pad Thai or Vermicelli!"

Q "**Off campus dining is really good**. It's Houston. There are lots of restaurants here. Some of my personal favorites in the village are Ruggles, La Madeline, Kin's Cafe, and Quiznos."

Q "There are an abundance of excellent restaurants for a plethora of moods and occasions in the downtown area. **Popular late-night destinations include Taco Cabana and the legendary House of Pies**. On the opposite end of the scale, upscale restaurants like Masraff's and Americas provide unbelievably good food and an incomparable atmosphere for the finest in fine dining."

Q "**The restaurants in the Village, and in Houston in general, are great**. Some good spots close by are Two Rows, Texadelphia, Istanbul Grill, Miss Saigon Café, Ruggles Café and Bakery, Goode Company Texas Seafood, 59 Diner, and Houston's."

Q "Excellent. **Houston's restaurant scene is basically unrivalled in the USA**, with cuisine ranging from BBQ, to simply TexMex, to Ethiopian."

Q "There are a billion great Houston restaurants cheap enough for students—discover your own! My favorites include Brasil (for coffee and food), Barnaby's (the location on Fairview is more fun and funky than the one on Montrose), Paulie's (for good vegetarian fare), Empire Cafe (Tuesday night is half-price cake night), Chapultipec is open late and has good margaritas. **Everyone has a preferred Mexican restaurant in Houston**. There's also Yan Sushi (also known as sushi-to-go and the sushi cube) and Bubba's (a buffalo burger shack). There are a lot of restaurants open all night or near to it—Mai's Vietnamese, Taco Cabana, IHOP, and the ever-popular House of Pies."

The College Prowler Take On...
Off-Campus Dining

The dining options in Houston are absolutely amazing. There is a rumor that Houston has more restaurants per capita than any other city in the United States, with the possible exception of NYC. Houston restaurants will impress with quantity, quality, and diversity. Nearby Rice Village is home to a variety of dining establishments, including everything from Mexican, Spanish tapas, bar and grill food, Scottish pub, Turkish, Indian, Chinese, Thai, smoothies and crepes, Mediterranean, and French food. Venture up Kirby or down Montrose for many more nearby options. China Town is worth the drive for excellent Asian cuisine or for ever-so-tasty Tapioca Pearl Drinks (a popular snack with Rice students). For higher scale dining, the Galleria district offers some excellent options, although nice restaurants can be found closer to campus, as well.

Of course, the Texas location means that a good (or at least cheap) Tex-Mex restaurant is located every few blocks. However, the diverse population of the large city means that you can also find just about any other type of cuisine that you might be craving, and some you would never even think of! Look around online, ask Houston natives or upperclassmen, or just get in your car and drive until you find a place that catches your eye.

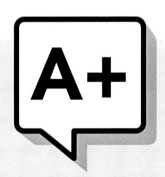

The College Prowler® Grade on

Off-Campus
Dining: A+

A high Off-Campus Dining grade implies that off campus restaurants are affordable, accessible, and worth visiting. Other factors include the variety of cuisine and the availability of alternative options (vegetarian, vegan, kosher, etc.).

Campus Housing

The Lowdown On...
Campus Housing

Room Types:
Residence rooms include singles, doubles, and suites.

Undergrads Living on Campus:
80%

Best Dorms:
Jones College

Wiess College

Number of Dormitories:
9

Worst Dorms:
Lovett

Number of University-Owned Apartments:
1

Dormitories:

Baker College
Named for Captain James Addison Baker, attorney for William Marsh Rice and first chair of the Rice Board of Trustees

6320 Main Street, Houston, TX 77005

vfrazier@rice.edu

http://bakercollege.net/about/index.jsp

Special: It was the first of the residential colleges, has a beautiful commons, a strong tradition of Fall musicals and spring Shakespeare productions, and a few good parties (Baker Blues, Kicker Party, Bakerfeast), starting point of the infamous Baker 13 (*see Rice Traditions section*).

Brown College
Named for Margaret Root Brown, wife of Rice benefactor Herman Brown, who established The Brown Foundation, and gave many other major gifts to Rice

9 Sunset Blvd., Houston, TX 77005

brown@rice.edu

www.brown.rice.edu

Special: It has a new wing and commons, is attached to one of the new serveries, has student parking directly behind the building, and a few good parties (Margaritaville, Bacchanalia).

Hanszen College
Named for Harry Clay Hanszen, benefactor and former chair of the Rice Board of Trustees

6350 Main Street, Houston, TX 77005

hans@rice.edu

http://hc.hanszen.rice.edu/

Special: It just got a new commons and is attached to one of the new serveries, has a strong tradition of Fall musicals, known for having the worst cheers of any college, and traditionally sponsors "Mardi Gras Night," a party that features—among other things—a strip-tease contest.

Jones College
Named for Mary Gibbs Jones, wife of Rice benefactor Jesse H. Jones.

23 Sunset Blvd., Houston, TX 77005

jone@rice.edu

www.rice.edu/projects/colleges/jones/

Special: It just got a new residential wing and new commons, is attached to one of the new serveries, has a strong Beer Bike and IM sports tradition, and is known for throwing some of the best private parties on campus.

Lovett College
Named for Edgar Odell Lovett, first president of The Rice Institute

6310 Main Street, Houston, TX 77005

harp@rice.edu

http://eol.lovett.rice.edu/

Special: It looks like a toaster—really (It was built to be riot-proof)! Lovett has a strong tradition of fall & spring theater, formerly had the dirtiest cheers on campus, is home to The Undergrounds (a cool, cozy, free student music venue), and throws "Casino Night" every year.

Martel College
Named for Marian and Speros Martel, whose foundation has a tradition of philanthropy to the University

99 Sunset Blvd., Houston, TX 77005

maria@rice.edu

www.ruf.rice.edu/%7emartel/index.html

Special: It is the newest college and has a new building and commons, is attached to one of the new serveries, was formed by volunteer transfer students from each of the other colleges, and is still in the first stages of discovering its traditions and identity as a college.

Sid Richardson College
Named for Sidney Williams Richardson, Rice benefactor

6360 Main Street, Houston, TX 77005

sid@rice.edu

www.sidrich.net/

Special: It is the tallest building on campus, has a strong tradition of Spring musicals, purposefully and creatively forfeits Beer Bike every year, throws some of the most well-attended parties on campus ('80s Party and Tower Party).

Wiess College
Named for Harry Carothers Wiess, Rice benefactor and trustee

6340 Main Street, Houston, TX 77005

wiess@rice.edu

www.rice.edu/projects/colleges/wiess/

Special: It just got a whole new building and a new commons, is attached to one of the new serveries, has a strong IM sports and theater tradition, prides itself on doing things differently from the other colleges (O-week and Beer Bike never have themes, only one college cheer), owns a huge flying pig,and is home to NOD (Night of Decadence).

Will Rice College
Named for William M. Rice, Jr., Rice benefactor and trustee and nephew of founder William Marsh Rice

6330 Main Street, Houston, TX 77005

wrc@rice.edu

http://phoenix.wrc.rice.edu

Special: It has a strong Beer Bike tradition (they have taken home the men's, women's, AND alumni race on more than one occasion, leading to the cheer "Will Rice will sweep!"), almost always win the Alumni race, and have a strong tradition of fall musicals.

Residential Colleges

Rice University operates on the Residential College system. Every incoming student is randomly assigned to one of the nine residential colleges. Students are not allowed to request a specific college unless they are a legacy student (had a close relative that attended Rice). Legacy students may only request that they be placed in the same college as their relative, or that they be placed in any of the other eight colleges. All of the nine colleges are coed, and the majority have only coed floors. Most of the colleges have their own laundry facilities (the price is covered in your housing fees), commons (dining hall), small library, weight room, game room, music practice rooms, and storage area. Each of the colleges also offers a unique personality, social scene, history, traditions, cheers, and much more.

Bed Type

Twin extra-long (39"x80"); some lofts, some bunk-beds

Cleaning Service?

Cleaning service in all bathrooms (communal and suite) and public areas.

What You Get

Each student receives a bed, dresser, desk, desk chair, bookshelf, lamp, ladder, Internet access, cable.

Also Available

Single-sex floors are available on request.

Did You Know?

The Rice residential college is modeled off of the system originated in Great Britain (**Oxford and Cambridge still have the residential college system**). Other U.S. universities with the residential college system include Harvard and Yale.

Students Speak Out On...
Campus Housing

{ **"The dorms are great. You don't have a choice, so you can't avoid any one over another. They all have their pros and cons, but generally they are very nice places to live."**

Q "Compared to other universities, **Rice housing is virtually luxurious**."

Q "**I don't live in a dorm. I live in a Residential College**. The residential college system creates buildings that are more than just a dorm. They house my friends, my 'Rice family,' my sports team, my theatre productions, my servery, my laundry facility, my computer lab, my pool table, my hammock, and my livelihood. It is a microcosm of Rice, but without the academics. It is my home away from home. It's why I chose Rice."

Q "You get assigned to a college which you'll (theoretically) live in for all four years. Martel is the newest, and **it has all suites, which is a good thing**. From what I hear, Will Rice has the worst rooms, though they do have a good social atmosphere there, so that makes up for it."

Q "I like all the colleges. Martel is the newest. **All are supposed to be equal, but they aren't really** because they were all built at different times, and they all have different amenities."

"The dorms are pretty nice. I've only ever lived in Jones College, and at this point the thought of sharing a small bedroom with someone is intolerable, but **the singles there are nice and spacious** and new suites were just built a few years ago. I think all the dorms have something to offer. The north campus dorms are comparatively, inconveniently located further away from most academic buildings, but the whole campus only takes about 20 minutes to walk across, so the difference isn't as great as it is made out to be."

"When you go to Rice, you're pseudo-randomly assigned to a college so that there's an even mix of students between the colleges. **Not all of the dorms are the same** quality, but most rooms on campus are pretty nice."

"The dorms are mostly really nice. We all live in residential colleges, which I think is **the best thing about being at Rice**. Your college is your family for four years. You live with these people, eat with them, study with them, and form lasting friendships with them. Everyone is assigned randomly to a college when they first enroll at Rice, so all of the colleges are very diverse and full of people from different backgrounds, hobbies, interests, and majors. We also have Masters and Residential Advisors (RAs) who are faculty members that live here at the colleges with us. They serve as our liaisons to the administration, as well as being adults we can go to for advice and support. They're not at all like parents, more like favorite aunts and uncles or close family friends."

"Basically, all of the residential colleges are nice—some are a little newer than others, and each has a different culture and spirit—but **since you're randomly assigned to one, it's not really something to choose**. And whichever one you get assigned to, you'll become convinced that it's the best."

Q "The living situation varies from college to college and even within colleges, but overall, Rice does a great job of taking care of its students. All forms of rooms are available—suites, hall-style bathrooms, doubles, singles, single sex, coed, and more. It just depends on what college you're in. The rooms are generally quite spacious compared to those at other universities, and all necessary furniture is provided. **Room choice almost always gets better as one gets older**, and you acquire more room draw points. So, by senior year, you almost certainly will not be disappointed."

The College Prowler Take On...
Campus Housing

Rice students tend to be very pleased with campus living and the residential colleges. Unlike most universities, you do not get to pick your dorm at Rice. As an incoming student you will be randomly assigned to a college, and most students stay at this college until graduation. You will be associated with the college even while living off campus. Transferring between colleges is an option, but no more than a handful of students take this route. Students are more likely to move "deep OC (off campus)" if they are highly dissatisfied with their college.

Each residential college becomes something like a family unit, and each has a special personality, spirit, and unique traditions. During freshman orientation week, freshman advisors have a high success rate of thoroughly brainwashing the newbie students into believing that their college is head and shoulders above all the other colleges. The buildings themselves vary because they were built with different architectural styles and at different times. Some colleges have been lucky enough to have new buildings in the last two years (Martell and Wiess), others have a new residential wing (Brown and Jones) and others have gotten a new commons and servery (Hanszen, Wiess, Jones, Martell, and Brown).

The College Prowler® Grade on

Campus Housing: A

A high Campus Housing grade indicates that dorms are clean, well-maintained and spacious. Other determining factors include variety of dorms, proximity to classes and social atmosphere.

Off-Campus Housing

The Lowdown On...
Off-Campus Housing

Undergrads in Off-Campus Housing:

20%

Average Rent For:

Studio Apt.: $545 month
1BR Apt.: $638 month
2BR Apt.: $689 month

Best Time to Look for a Place:

August–September

Popular Areas:

West University

University Place

Inner Loop

For Assistance Contact

The Off-Campus Housing Office

https://sturec.rice.edu/stucent/housing/index.asp

(713) 348-4096

OCH@rice.edu

Students Speak Out On...
Off-Campus Housing

"Off-campus housing is easy, cheap and close. The Houston housing market is one of the cheapest in the country, although the University is in one of the nicest parts of town."

Q "If it had been possible for me to live on campus all four years, I would have done it, but I lived off campus my junior year, and it was fun, too. **The apartment scene around Rice is great**. It's reasonable, and there are lots of places really close to Rice so that you can still stay involved on campus."

Q "There are quite a few apartment complexes relatively close to Rice that cater to students, and most are quite nice. **Living off campus can be cheaper** and more private, but many students prefer to live on campus throughout their time at Rice. I personally feel that living off campus results in losing touch with what is happening at Rice, and it tends to limit social interaction to classes and special occasions. I also think that the social element of college is a very important one, and this is a time that will never come around again. A person has the rest of his or her life to live in apartments, but it remains a question of personal preference, and strong arguments can be made for both sides."

Q "Rice only guarantees housing for three of the four years, and the majority of the students live on-campus for three or four years. **Rice is, by no means, a commuter school**, and with the Residential College system, most people want to stay on campus to be active within the Rice community."

Q "**I was against the idea of living off campus**, but I got booted my sophomore year. I found that it was difficult to keep up with my old social circles, since a lot of them were on campus or spread out in different apartment complexes. However, it turned out to be a very positive thing because I branched out into new social circles, explored new parts of Houston, and gained some valuable life experience. It was one of my favorite semesters at Rice!"

Q "I don't have any experience with living off campus, but from what I've heard and my observations, people living off campus tend to **have a harder time making themselves go to class**, and they get less and less involved with their college as time goes on."

Q "**I love living off campus**. It gives me a place to go home to, but it also allows me to always go back to my college and feel at home. You do have to make more of an effort to keep in touch with people, though."

Q "It depends. **As a freshmen, you are required to live your first year on campus**. Off-campus housing can be quite convenient should you have the means to live close to campus—this usually means finding an apartment within five minutes of campus. All of these complexes are expensive, but with roommates, they're affordable. The further away from campus, the less convenient."

Q "**You will definitely need a car** if you want to live off campus. But why would you? Colleges are so much fun."

Q "We're right in the middle of things—there are dozens of apartment complexes. **It's not a question of finding; it's a question of choosing**."

Q "It's totally worth it, in my opinion. Living off campus as a student is a great way to **mitigate the conflict between wanting privacy and not wanting isolation**—there's always a couch to sleep on if you want to sleep on campus some weekend, and if you get a meal plan you can still have lunches between classes at your residential college. Also, living off campus is the best way I know to get to know Houston—-most of the cool places that made me love living there I'd never been to before I moved off, and some of the best friends I made at Rice were friends I met that year. The best way to go about it is to find somewhere within walking distance (there are a few) and to move off with someone that you're good friends with already."

Q "I've lived in off campus housing for three years, but **I've always been an active part** of the on-campus social scene. There is a nice neighborhood around Rice, as well as many apartment complexes, but bring a car."

Q "Off-campus housing is cheaper than living on campus, but the drawback is that you generally need to have a car, and parking is going up in price every year. However, the experience of living off campus is generally worth it, because it's really great to have your own room, be able to cook your own food, and feel free to do what you want to do when you want to do it. Plus, if you move off voluntarily, **you get Voluntary Move-Off Points**, which means you can never get bumped off campus again, and you get extra points in the room draw for the rest of your time at Rice. This can even be fulfilled by going abroad for a semester or a year (which I also highly recommend)."

The College Prowler Take On...
Off-Campus Housing

Many students try to stay on campus for their entire time at Rice because Rice's social life is so focused on campus and within the college system. Some students feel that living off campus cuts them off from their old social circles, making it hard for them to keep up with their friends or make new friends. Other students feel quite the opposite, seeing living off campus as a breath of fresh air and a break from the monotony of campus living, the college system, the same social hangouts and activities, and the same parties. They have found off-campus life to be a very positive experience, and feel that is has widened their social circle and helped them to get out and explore Houston.

As for the housing selections off campus, there is a huge variety to choose from, including actual houses, apartments, townhouses, garage apartments, and studio apartments. A range of prices are available, and apartments can be found very near to campus (a must if you will not have a car), as well as farther away. The online Off-Campus Housing Guide is a very helpful resource to see what is currently available, and if you start looking early (a few months in advance), you should not have any problem finding a place to your liking.

The College Prowler® Grade on

Off-Campus Housing: A-

A high grade in Off-Campus Housing indicates that apartments are of high quality, close to campus, affordable, and easy to secure.

Diversity

The Lowdown On...
Diversity

African American:
7%

White:
64%

Asian American:
15%

International:
2%

Hispanic:
11%

Out-of-State:
47%

Native American:
1%

Political Activity

Rice students and faculty tend to be politically liberal, although there is an outspoken conservative minority. In general, the number of students who are politically active is very small, although there have been a handful of issues at Rice that led to large protests and high student interest. While the conservative student might feel out of place in the average political discussion, students are respectful of all differing opinions, and intelligent debate is usually welcome.

Gay Pride

While there are always exceptions, the student body as a whole is very tolerant and usually very accepting of all sexual orientations. There is support provided through organizations such as ALLY, Pride, the Rice Counseling Center, and Minority Affairs. The city of Houston also has a sizeable and very visible gay community.

Economic Status

There is a stereotype that Rice students come from wealthy families, but this is generally unfounded. Rice is known to be a "best-buy" university, and people from all socio-economic backgrounds attend. The student body mixes well enough that economic differences are rarely visible.

Most Popular Religions

Organizations or representatives of all major religions can be found at Rice. The most outspoken and visible religious organizations are Christian and include Campus Crusade, InterVarsity Christian Fellowship, and the Catholic Student Association. The Jewish organization on campus, Hillel, is small but fairly active. The Houston area provides a variety of churches and worship centers for various faiths and denominations.

Minority Clubs

In addition to the Black Student Association (BSA) and the Hispanic Association for Cultural Enrichment at Rice (HACER), Rice offers individual clubs for most Asian minorities (Indian Students at Rice, Korean Student Association, Asian Pacific Americans for Social Action (APASA), South Asian Society, Chinese Student Association, Taiwanese Association, Vietnamese Association), as well as other cultural or minority organizations (Iranian Society, Turkish Student Association, Ruz [which translates into Rice in Arabic], Native American Student Association). The majority of these clubs sponsor social and cultural events throughout the year, most of which are open to the entire student body. These events include holiday festivals, study breaks, fashion shows, and themed dance nights.

Students Speak Out On...
Diversity

"Diversity does exist, but not that much since it's a highly expensive school. Mostly, you will see whites and Asian students on campus."

"**Rice is pretty diverse**. People of all different ethnicities, political viewpoints, religious beliefs, sexual orientations, and economic backgrounds come to Rice. The general attitude on campus seems to be that everyone has the right to do their own thing and not be bothered about it."

"Rice is, all in all, a good place to come out and discover/experiment with your sexuality. **Students do try to embrace differences**. Occasionally, however, the conservative values of the surroundings prevail, making it seem like all the talk of gay tolerance is really nothing more than lip service."

"**Rice is not very diverse, I don't think**. I grew up in a diverse town, so it didn't really impress me. In general, I'd say the campus is certainly liberal, and it embraces all different backgrounds and ethnicities, but I can't really say statistically what the population breakdown is."

"Rice is pretty diverse. There are a lot of Hispanics, African Americans, and Asians. We also have a pretty large international population. However, **the campus is still mostly white**, both among the students and faculty."

Q "**Rice is very sexually diverse, which may or may not scare you**. We also have lots of minorities, but in Texas there is no affirmative action, so there are no minorities here just because they're minorities. Although there is often a perception that rich, white, prep-school students make up the student body, I would beg to differ, and say that they are a very small percentage. Rice is made up of mostly middle- to upper-middle class students."

Q "Rice is a fairly diverse campus. **It's not as diverse as some schools**, but it has its share of different people. And there are definitely people from all kinds of different backgrounds—religions, home state (and country), urban, rural, and more."

Q "It depends on where you are coming from. There are definitely representatives from all different cultural groups at Rice and clubs that promote both cultural unity and awareness. **I was surprised by how few African American students there were at Rice**, but there are a decent number of Asian, Indian, and Hispanic Students."

Q "Rice is highly diverse, with significant numbers of nearly **every conceivable type of minority**. Especially prevalent are those with backgrounds from all corners of Asia. Numerous clubs and associations exist to provide people of all races with a chance to explore other cultures and participate in traditional events."

Q "We're big on diversity. There are all sorts of people on campus, and all sorts of racial groups, political groups, and different sexual orientations. There's plenty to get involved in—**Rice is pretty open to anything**. You'll make a lot of diverse friends, but of course, only if you want to."

The College Prowler Take On...
Diversity

Student opinion on diversity at Rice depends largely on previous individual experiences. Students who come from homogenous hometowns or high schools find Rice to be extremely diverse, while students from large cities have felt disappointed by the lack of diversity at Rice. It is true that representatives can be found from nearly any political, social, racial, ethnic, sexual, or religious group, and many of these groups sponsor various clubs and organizations on campus. The level of involvement and visibility of these clubs varies, but some are extremely involved and sponsor study breaks and/or holiday or cultural celebrations with the intent to share their beliefs and culture with the entire student body.

Many students would criticize campus diversity, however, in that Hispanics and African Americans seem to be underrepresented, and many groups tend to segregate themselves, to some extent. At any rate, the expression of intolerance or prejudice against any minority group is strongly frowned upon, and Rice is a fairly liberal place (despite it's conservative Texan setting). Students can feel free to speak their mind, express their beliefs, and be proud of who they are and where they come from.

The College Prowler® Grade on

Diversity: B

A high grade in Diversity indicates that ethnic minorities and international students have a notable presence on campus, and that students of different economic backgrounds, religious beliefs, and sexual preferences are well-represented.

Guys & Girls

The Lowdown On...
Guys & Girls

Women Undergrads:
49%

Men Undergrads:
51%

Birth Control Available?
Yes. Student Health Services, Residential College Health Representatives

Social Scene

One absolutely brilliant aspect of Rice University is the college system, because it takes a large incoming class of intelligent, and often socially awkward, people and breaks it down into subgroups (residential colleges). It gives freshmen an instant social network. During orientation week, a group of randomly selected and diverse individuals are given something in common—Jones College (or Baker College or Lovett College, or Wiess College. They go through the same indoctrination process, have the same pranks played on them by upperclassmen, go on the same scavenger hunt, sit through the same boring meetings, and so on. They meet the College Masters (a faculty family that lives in a house adjoining or near to their building), and discover that they have a set of parents and (usually) young siblings provided for them.

The college system makes the big step of making first social connections upon entering the University a piece of cake. Some people feel that this can be a downside if students never choose to go beyond the walls of their own residential college. This isn't entirely negative, since each college consists of a very diverse population. However, the social scene can begin to feel limited by the end of sophomore year if a student doesn't make an attempt venture out. Luckily, there are tons of easy ways to meet people at Rice if a person feels inclined to do so. Social involvement runs the gamut from social recluses who lock themselves away with their computers every day, to social butterflies who seem to know every face they see on campus.

Hookups or Relationships?

The running joke is that people come in as freshmen and either meet someone during orientation week, date them for four years and then get married, or they will experience nothing more than late-night party hookups for four years. The truth is that Rice students do tend to stick to committed relationships or hookups, and the latter is slightly more popular than the former. In short, not much casual dating goes on here.

Did You Know?

Top Places to Find Hotties:	**Top Places to Hook Up:**
1. Parties/Pub	1. Single dorm rooms
2. Library	2. 180° statue
3. Autry Court	3. Library study rooms
	4. Parties
	5. Laundry rooms

Best Place to Meet Guys/Girls

An overwhelming majority of Rice relationships and hookups occur within the walls of each residential college. Many colleges have unofficial "hookup webs" that map out the degrees of separation between the members of that college. Relationships within a residential college are easiest to get into, and most convenient, because you live in the same building, eat in the same servery, hang out in the same lobbies and quad areas, and attend a lot of the same social events. The downside is that rumors run rampant within each college.

Relationships that occur between students from different colleges are most often sparked because of a common interest or mutual membership in a class, club, religious group, or other. People may meet through athletics, theater, the Outdoors Club, the Engineering Club, swing dancing class, English 101, or any number of campus activities.

Dress Code

The looks at Rice range from preppy, to athletic, to thrift store. Clothes are just one of many ways that Rice students find to express themselves. People tend to find what works for them and makes them comfortable, and develop their own style. There are girls that dress up in skirts and curl their hair every day, while other students regularly go to class in sweats or hospital scrubs. Anything goes!

Students Speak Out On...
Guys & Girls

> "The saying around here goes: 'Brains before beauty at Rice University.'"

"Rice is pretty dorky at first glance, but there are a lot of amazing, interesting, intense, and yes, beautiful people out there. If you're not meeting them at big college parties, **try looking at off-campus parties**, Rice theater events, and student organizations. I don't think it's really possible to characterize the entire male or female population of the school, but there is definitely someone out there looking for what you are looking for, whether that is a serious, deep relationship or a hookup. You'll probably run into the latter more often than you'd like, but the former is entirely possible and likely within a student body as diversely talented as rice. I recommend the architecture students, personally."

"There are attractive as well as unattractive people everywhere. **People will tell you that Rice has a shortage of good-looking students**, but Rice is such a small school. You don't really pick your friends. It's more like you're presented with about 100 of them at your dorm the day you get here, and you will know all 100 very well when you graduate together. At that point, looks really cease to matter."

"The students (though not all of them) can tend to be somewhat geeky. As a whole, **most aren't 'hot,' although they're definitely out there**. For the most part, they're just fun and stimulating to be with—for staying up with 'til 5 a.m. talking, studying, partying, or having a fun, late-night Houston expedition."

Q "**You aren't going to find any incredibly beautiful people with nothing substantial about them at Rice**. Everyone here is intelligent—everyone here cares about or is passionate about something. The amount of dating that goes on might be less than at larger schools, maybe because many students sometimes limit themselves to their own residential colleges when looking for a significant other. One unfortunate thing about that is that everyone will soon know all the messy details of the hookup/relationship. One thing is certain, Rice guys are much less aggressive/assertive than your average college guy. If a Rice guy asks you out on an actual date, then that is a pretty impressive thing."

Q "Everyone at Rice is weird and is a nerd in his or her own way. So **there's no fear of sticking out** because of that. It's easy to meet people you get along with, have great conversations with, and can relate to on an intellectual level. However, it's hard to meet people you want to have a relationship with."

Q "Rice is small. You end up knowing a lot of people. This tends to limit the dating pool. Most people at Rice are actively searching for a significant other, and at the same time, no one really has the time to invest in a healthy relationship. On the other hand, **it seems like most couples you find are either hookups or long-term relationships**. It's really quite confusing. Rice also has a very high intermarriage rate after graduation. I've heard that as many as 70 percent of Rice grads marry other Rice grads (although they didn't have to be dating while they were students here). So, in general, there seems to be some hope for finding someone at Rice, but it may be down the road after graduation. Dating while here doesn't seem to be all that successful for most people."

Q "**Rice guys joke that there are no cute girls on campus, and vice versa**. I don't know how true that is. It seems that many Rice students don't feel like they need to take lots of time getting ready for class in the morning, but I think that most Rice students clean up nice."

Q "**At least the guys are already smart**—they have that going for them. They can be somewhat socially inept, though, because they are not used to dating. They're used to studying. One thing that is awesome about this, though, is that you can develop awesome relationships with guys because they are really good friends. So many guys will become like brothers to you, and that is really cool. I think there are hot guys. But it's the type of 'hot' that comes from getting to know a guy honestly. There are no 'hot state school guys,' so you won't see models strolling around campus, but you will meet a lot of really cool people with the same values and aspirations you might have."

Q "**Not necessarily 'hot,'** but there are enough attractive people around campus. And most people you meet are amazingly interesting—I have friends who major in all kinds of different fields, which leads to some fun conversations. I continue to be amazed by how much some of my friends know."

Q "First, you must understand that the guys and girls at Rice are all very intelligent people at the minimum. Now, standard stereotypes would customarily dictate that all such people compensate for this gift with decreased social skills and general unattractiveness. There are plenty of jokes based on this concept told by those inside and outside of Rice, and it is a popular thing for students to complain about, as students everywhere will do. In my opinion, although there definitely are those who conform to, and help perpetuate, that stereotype, **there are quite a good number of attractive girls** who also happen to be really cool and a lot of fun."

The College Prowler Take On...
Guys & Girls

The widely-circulated, and not entirely unsubstantiated, rumor is that Rice students tend to be unattractive, and that the only two kinds of Rice relationships are random hookups or four-year relationships that eventually lead to marriage. The truth is that the dating situation and experience at Rice varies for everyone. You may not find as many traditionally attractive hotties at Rice as you would at large state schools, but then again, we have fewer people. We tend not to attract many stereotypical "frat boys or sorority girls," although there are a few, and the number may be increasing. This has been attributed to an issue of *Seventeen* magazine, which declared Rice the number one choice school "for girls who want it all."

Rumor has it that the number of attractive ladies on campus has gone up this year, perhaps as a result of the article's claim that Rice offers cute guys of all types. You can, of course, find whatever "type" you might be looking for (or not looking for) at Rice: athletic, romantic, poetic, intelligent, flirtatious, theatrical, intelligent, geeky, genuine, graceful, player, intelligent, elegant, boy/girl-next-door . . .

The College Prowler® Grade on Guys: C+

A high grade for Guys indicates that the male population on campus is attractive, smart, friendly, and engaging, and that the school has a decent ratio of guys to girls.

The College Prowler® Grade on Girls: C

A high grade for Girls not only implies that the women on campus are attractive, smart, friendly, and engaging, but also that there is a fair ratio of girls to guys.

Athletics

The Lowdown On...
Athletics

Athletic Division:
NCAA Division I-A

Conference:
Conference USA

School Mascot:
Owls

**Men Playing
Varsity Sports:**
205 (8%)

**Women Playing
Varsity Sports:**
118 (6%)

➔

Men's Varsity Sports:
Baseball
Basketball
Cross-Country
Football
Golf
Tennis
Track & Field

Women Varsity Sports:
Basketball
Cross-Country
Track & Field
Tennis
Soccer
Swimming
Volleyball
Golf
Surfing

Club Sports:
Badminton
Cricket
Cycling
Fast Pitch (women's)
Fencing
Lacrosse
Outdoor Club
Power lifting
Rowing
Rugby
Sailing

(Club Sports, continued)
Skydiving
Soccer
Social Dance Society
Ultimate Frisbee
Volleyball
Water Polo
Wrestling

Intramurals:
Badminton
Basketball
Billiards
Cross Country
Disc Golf
Flag Football
Floor Hockey
Golf
Inner Tube Water Polo
Racquetball
Sand Volleyball
Soccer
Softball
Swimming
Table tennis
Tennis
Track
Ultimate Frisbee
Volleyball
Wallyball

Athletic Fields:
Reckling Park
Track/Soccer Stadium
Rice Stadium

Getting Tickets

Tickets to all Rice athletic events are free to Rice students with a valid student ID, and finding an available seat is never much of a problem.

Most Popular Sports

Baseball and football are without a doubt the most popular and widely supported sports at Rice University. Students rarely attend other sporting events, but every football game has a decent turnout. Since Rice won the 2003 College World Series (with the biggest victory in College World Series championship-game history), Rice students have suddenly become huge baseball fanatics.

Best Place to Take a Walk

Remember this phrase: Outer loop during the day, Inner loop at night.

Overlooked Teams

Every team other than football and baseball!

Gyms/Facilities

Autry Court
Autry Court is the main athletic facility on campus. It has a swimming pool, several full-sized basketball courts (volleyball and badminton nets are set up at certain times), racquetball courts, and two weight rooms. One of the rooms has strictly weights and weightlifting machines, the other has some weightlifting machines, as well as step-machines, rowing machines, exercise bikes, elliptical machines, and treadmills. Most of these machines are equipped with their own small-screen TVs. Bring your own headphones if you want sound!

Cox Fitness Center
A large facility with many weight and exercise machines, the Cox Fitness Center is located on the southeast corner of Rice Stadium, and is utilized by all Rice athletes, as well as some other members of the Rice community.

College Weight Rooms
Most of the residential colleges have small weight rooms of their own. These vary in quality, but the average college weight room has only a few standard machines (treadmill, step-machine, exercise bike, basic weights).

Outdoor Tennis Courts
There are outdoor tennis courts in two different locations on campus. Both facilities are very well-maintained and are lighted for nighttime play.

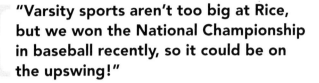

Students Speak Out On...
Athletics

"Varsity sports aren't too big at Rice, but we won the National Championship in baseball recently, so it could be on the upswing!"

Q "Support of varsity sports is virtually non-existent, but **IM sports are big**."

Q "Despite the fact that Rice is a Division I school, varsity athletics are not followed as much as at other Division I schools. However, IM sports are huge, especially when Residential colleges are pitted against each other. **Most students participate in IM sports** as players or fans. It's a great feeling being out on the field and having friends from your college cheer you on to victory."

Q "IM sports are big. Not a lot of people go to sports games. You won't find intense school spirit here for sports. **Most people don't have the time to go to them; they're always busy studying**."

Q "Varsity sports on campus are taken fairly seriously, but are not the epitome of college life. **Rice football is followed by most students**, as is Rice baseball, but other sports are usually followed sparsely. IM sports are taken fairly seriously, and many students actually do partake in them actively."

Q "**Not many people care** much about varsity sports on campus, except baseball. IM sports are pretty popular, as are college sports when the colleges compete against each other."

Q "Rice is Division I, but not very good. Many people go to football games, and our baseball team is ranked highly in the country. However, there are not a whole lot of varsity athletes around. IM sports are very good. There is a team for everything, and **just about everyone plays something**. They're a lot of fun."

Q "Varsity sports are pretty big, since we are a Division I school. However, most of our varsity teams are not exactly top-ranked, except for the baseball team, which won the 2003 College World Series for the first time in Rice history. Besides varsity sports, though, club, intramural, and college sport participation is huge. We have **one of the highest sport participation rates** in the country because there are so many options to choose from. By far, though, most people participate in the college sports. All of the residential colleges compete against each other for the President's Cup, so everyone wants to support his or her college and get outside and away from work for a while. Plus it's no pressure, and no experience is necessary to play in club and IM sports."

Q "**They are as big or small as you want them to be**. Rice is all about individuality. I don't play."

Q "IM sports are a lot more popular. There are actually club sports, intramural sports, and college sports for all of those who like to play but do not want the varsity commitment. **You can try things you've never done** or compete relatively seriously at sports you may play at the varsity level now. The recreation center is working on making improvements to the fitness and cardio rooms."

Q "The majority of students are **pretty apathetic when it comes to the varsity teams**. However, I have been to some of the varsity sporting events, and it is fun when you know certain players from your college, or if you go with a student group to support."

Q "IM sports are big, but there are **no big varsity sports**, in my opinion."

Q "The school is Division I, but most sports aren't a huge deal. IMs are really big though—many students participate in something, and **we have a huge assortment of IMs**."

Q "IM sports are pretty big, but varsity is not. **Sports are not all that big** here, although we do have teams."

Q "Sports are not that big here. **There are a lot of intramurals**. It's probably because the fields are along the outskirts of the campus, so we don't get to see the athletes."

Q "**Varsity sport events are usually not as well attended at Rice** as they tend to be at other schools. Rice is the smallest school in the country that competes at the Division I level, which means that we are always competing against opponents with a much greater pool of students to draw from. A classic example is when Rice plays the University of Texas—a school of 2,700 taking on a 50,000 student powerhouse. But despite this disadvantage, Rice actually does quite well in most sports, and phenomenally well in a select few. Women's basketball, as well as men's and women's cross-country, track, and tennis are a few sports in which Rice excels."

Q "The men's baseball team recently defied all odds to win the College World Series in 2003 for the first time ever, toppling Texas—not once but twice—before defeating Stanford in the final. **There is also a good IM sports program with an amazingly wide selection of activities**, including oddities like wallyball and, get this, inner tube water polo!"

The College Prowler Take On...
Athletics

As the smallest Division I school in the country, we always play against bigger schools, which unfortunately has not resulted in a fabulous athletic record. Despite being Division I, students do not demonstrate much school spirit or support in regards to Rice's varsity teams. Home football games usually get a fairly decent turnout, and after claiming the championship title of the College World Series in 2003 (Woo hoo!), the baseball team has since received massive support and attention. Sadly, most of our other varsity teams go virtually unnoticed by the overall student population. Compared to other universities that charge students to attend games and still fill the seats, Rice gives free tickets to any Rice student, and most athletic events still have poor attendance.

The club and intramural environment is another thing entirely. A large variety of club and intramural sports are available, and a high percentage of the student population participates on one of these teams. Competition between the residential colleges is what drives the intramural system (although non-team or non-college sports are also very popular). Powder-puff and Flag football games between colleges usually draw a crowd of fans/cheerleaders from the respective colleges. It could definitely be argued that more students on campus care about the club and intramural teams than the varsity teams.

The College Prowler® Grade on

Athletics: B-

A high grade in athletics indicates that students have school spirit, that sports programs are respected, that games are well-attended, and that intramurals are a prominent part of student life.

Nightlife

The Lowdown On...
Nightlife

Club and Bar Prowler:
Popular Nightlife Spots!

Club Crawler:

Houston has plenty of clubs, and regardless of your musical preferences, sexual preferences, style of dress, or age, you can probably find what you are looking for. Most clubs close between 2 and 3 a.m. Here are a few of the more popular clubs that are frequented by Rice students.

Elvia's International Restaurant and Club

2727 Fondren Road # 2A

(713) 266-9631

Elvia's is a full night out on the town! Start with an inexpensive Mexican meal and enjoy live music with big Latin bands or free flamenco shows every other Thursday night. Hit the dance floor right away, or if you'd rather polish up your Latin dance skills in advance, free Salsa lessons are given every Wednesday between 8 p.m. and 9 p.m.

➡

(Elvia's International Restaurant and Club, continued)

Happy hour Wednesday-Friday 6 p.m.–8 p.m.

Ladies night every Wednesday and Thursday.

Numbers

300 Westheimer Rd.

(713) 526-6551

/www.numbersnightclub.com

One of the most well-known clubs in Houston, Numbers opened in 1978 and has hosted concerts with big name stars such as The Village People, Nine Inch Nails, Elliot Smith, Snoop Dogg and Paul Oakenfold, as well as a variety of great local bands. Numbers caters to all ages and musical interests. Check out their Web site to learn about theme nights and events. If you get tired of dancing, you can take a break to play pool, a video game, watch either of the two giant video screens playing flash remix videos, or chill out and enjoy a drink at the second floor bar, which overlooks the dance floor below.

Tuesdays are sometimes Swing Night (check the schedule on the Web), Thursday is Goth Night, and Friday is '80s Night (50 cent Shiner).

Rich's

2401 San Jacinto St.

(713) 759-9606

www.richs-houston.com

Although many heterosexual females (and occasional heterosexual males) sometimes frequent Rich's to avoid sleazy come-ons and just have the opportunity to dance, the target crowd of this two-story club is Houston's young gay and lesbian population. Rich's is the home of Texas's largest dance floor on its main level. Many people use the upper level lounge area to take a break, watch the action happening on the dance floor below, enjoy a drink, or check out the decorations (artwork done by local artists). This is an intense club with a lively crowd. Dress to impress; 18 and older. While many club goers (gay and straight) would call this one of their favorite spots, a word of caution is to use the restroom before you go. The restrooms in the club are commonly used for "recreational activities" that make actually using the facilities an unpleasant experience!

The Roxy

5351 West Alabama & Rice Ave.

(713) 850-ROXY

http://www.clubroxy.com/

Located near the galleria, The Roxy is one of the more popular clubs in the area, and is open to anyone 18 or older, with lots of special deals for ladies or people over 21. Most nights have themes (Hip Hop, Latin, Retro, etc.), and the attire is dressier for some nights than others (check out the dress code online). The Roxy also hosts occasional concerts and contests, as well as special events such as foam parties. Live DJs spin 6 nights a week.

Tuesdays: Retro Active Tuesdays, 21 and older get in for free all night.

Wednesdays: No cover for ladies until 10 p.m., free deluxe buffet 7 p.m.-10 p.m.

Thursdays: No cover for ladies until 11 p.m., $1.50 drinks till 11 p.m., $2.50 wells after 11 p.m., hip hop and Latin house.

Friday: All ladies 21& up, no cover and 50 cent drinks from 9 p.m.-11 p.m.

Wild West

6101 Richmond Ave.

(713) 266-3455 or (713) 266-3480

http://www.wildwesthouston .com/index.asp

Wild West is considered the best two-stepping country club and bar in Houston. With a motto like "Two-Steppin and Longneckin'," you know you are in for a good time! In addition to the good times on the dance floor, you can shoot pool, play blackjack, or get your boots shined (no, I'm not kidding). The atmosphere is to die for—solid oak floor, lady bartenders in scandalous cowgirl outfits, and a large number of people of all ages wearing cowboy hats, boots, belt buckles! Don't worry if it is your first time; country/Texan attire is not required, and the DJs will break up the line dances and two-stepping with an occasional "booty break" of regular club music—at which time the dance floor usually clears of cowboys and is taken over by college students. People 21 and older usually have discounted cover charges, and drink specials can be found Tuesday-Sunday.

Thursday: $1.75 mixed drinks and most beer

Friday: $1.00 any drink in the house, all night long

Bar Prowler:

The bars in Houston are as numerous as the restaurants. You can find anything to fit your style, from your average run-of-the-mill sports bar with good deals on beer and wings to kooky places like Dean's Credit Clothing, which doubles as a thrift store. Here are a few of the most popular or most unique hangouts for the 21 and over crowd.

Ginger Man

5607 Morningside

(713) 526-2770

http://www.gingermanpub.com/

If you are looking for a laid-back atmosphere, and a pub that specializes in making beers, wines, and ciders, check out the Ginger Man. Usually not too crowded on weekdays, and within walking distance of Rice campus, this bar has a covered outdoor seating area with long wooden benches that make it a great place to go with a group of any size. It's never too noisy to have a good conversation at the Ginger Man, which makes it a popular spot with Rice students.

Valhalla

On Rice Campus

http://www.ruf.rice.edu/~bifrost/

Perhaps the most laid-back pub that you can possibly imagine, Valhalla is the graduate student pub, although it is also used by faculty, alumni, and upperclassmen that are over 21. The inside space is cozy, and it looks snazzier recently thanks to an awesome mural of Norse mythology in the entranceway. Valhalla is a non-profit organization, staffed entirely by volunteers, and the beer is cheap, my friends. The cool thing to do is go down into Valhalla (it is located beneath the old Chemistry Lecture Hall), buy your drinks, and bring them outside where you can drink leisurely on the steps of the Chem Lec building or the neighboring benches.

Volcano

2349 Bissonnet Street

(713) 526-5282

Another very popular place to ring in your 21st, this bar is located within walking distance from campus and has a great atmosphere with original decorations, outdoor seating, a tasty food menu, and delicious (but slightly pricey) mixed drinks. The beer selection isn't bad, but I highly recommend trying the Mojitos, Frozen Screwdrivers, or Strawberry Basil Margaritas.

Willy's Pub

On Rice Campus,
student center

(713) 348 4056

*http://www.ruf.rice.edu/
~willypub/*

The undergraduate campus
pub, Willy's Pub, is a great
place to hang out, grab a drink
or a bite to eat (smoothies,
pizza, and subs, popcorn,
chips), or play pool or darts.
Every Thursday night is
"Pub Night", and the place
gets crowded.

(Willy's Pub, continued)

The individual residential
colleges will usually sponsor
one pub night per semester
for their college specifically,
and on those nights college
members can usually get free
or discounted food and drink,
and karaoke is available.

Specials on Monday-Thursday
nights.

Other Places to Check Out

Dean's Credit Clothing

316 Main St., downtown

(713) 227-3326

www.deanscreditclothing.com

Dress to impress, or just buy something when you get here!
Dean's Credit Clothing is a classy bar/thrift store with great drink
selection, live music, and live fashion shows (or videos of fashion
shows playing on a big screen). Great atmosphere, but the music
sometimes gets loud enough to make conversation difficult.

Etta's Lounge

5120 Scott Street

(713) 528-2611

Bored on a Sunday night? Want something to do that is off the
beaten track? Etta's Lounge is a gold mine hidden away on Scott
Street, and it is frequented by very few college students. This jazz
and blues lounge also features greasy but tasty grill food and
buckets of cold beer, but the highlight is definitely the live music.
Every Sunday night there is an incredible line up of soulful singers
and bands. A small percentage of the crowd will sometimes take
to the dance floor, but many choose to just listen. Cover charge is
$5, and you must be 21 or older.

Houston Area Traditional Dance Society

www.hatds.org

board@hatds.org

This is not your every day ordinary dancing experience. This super friendly group of people organizes a traditional folk dance (called Contra Dancing) every other week, at a different Houston location. Cost is $4 or $5 with the student discount (and you'll get a coupon to let you come free for your second visit). This is the traditional dancing from movies: bow to your partner, swing your corner, and promenade. They have refreshments, a live caller and a live band, and they teach you the steps as you go. It's a great change of pace from the every day college hang out activities, and it is a lot of fun!

Marfreless

2006 Peden St., River Oaks

(713) 528-0083

Perfect for a romantic or potentially scandalous night out, this cozy lounge bar is hidden away behind an unmarked and inconspicuous blue door in the River Oaks district. This two-floor bar has a good selection of wines and champagne (the bubbly is brought out in fireman buckets, which is a very cool touch. However, if you try to swipe one, the management will get fairly upset). The downstairs is dimly lit, offers bar or table seating, and is used by the groups of platonic patrons. Upstairs, the lighting gets dimmer still, and faded couches are filled with couples getting comfortable. Venture further down the upstairs hallway and you will come to a room that is pitch black. What goes on in this room shall be left up to the imagination. Enter at your own risk . . .

West Alabama Ice House

1919 W Alabama St

(713) 528-6874

There's exclusively outdoor seating, very casual atmosphere, and a basketball court in the back!

Useful Resources for Nightlife:

www.houstonbeat.com

www.nightlife-houston.com

www.cityspin.com/houston/nitelife/nitelife.htm

Favorite Drinking Games:

Beer Pong

Beer Golf

Beer Cart

Card Games

Movie Drinking Games

Quarters

Kings

Cheapest Place to Get a Drink:

Campus Parties

Valhalla (beer)

Local Specialties:

Long Island Iced Teas (Marquis)

Margaritas

Lone Star

Student Favorites:

Willy's Pub

Valhalla

Ginger Man

Volcano

Wild Wild West

Numbers

The Roxy

Rich's

Bars Close At:

Most by 2 or 3 a.m.

Primary Areas with Nightlife:

The Rice Village

Downtown

Richmond Strip

Montrose

What to Do if You're Not 21

Good news for incoming freshmen: most clubs in Houston are 18 and older! Just bring a valid ID, and you shouldn't have a problem, although your cover charge might be slightly higher because you won't be forking out the dough for alcohol. Also, check out any of Houston's live music venues, including The Mausoleum or Brasil, both cute bars/coffeehouses with fun atmospheres and great performances by local groups. If drinks are what you crave, underclassmen can often get away with imbibing at Willy's Pub on campus (although the campus police have been known to make occasional busts, so drink at your own risk), campus parties (Campos are usually not a problem), or off-campus house parties. If drinking isn't your thing, Houston has tons of things to offer that don't require an over-21 ID. Check out the theater or museum districts, live concerts, sporting events, nearby Galveston beach, or get involved on campus!

Organization Parties

Most campus parties are sponsored by the different residential colleges. Small private parties might also be associated with different clubs, theatrical presentations (cast parties), sports teams (usually off-campus parties), and more. Once a year, the sophomore architecture students organize a huge party called "Archi Arts," which doubles as a fundraiser for their spring trip to Paris. Archi Arts is usually held in an original off-campus location and is always a themed costume party. The ticket price is fairly steep ($10-$12).

Frats

See the Greek section!

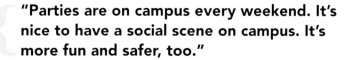
Students Speak Out On...
Nightlife

"Parties are on campus every weekend. It's nice to have a social scene on campus. It's more fun and safer, too."

Q "Rice has good parties, and there are good bars and clubs off campus. 'The Village' right behind the University has **a great number of excellent Houston bars** within walking distance."

Q "**The bar and club scene is like the restaurant scene**. There's a wide variety in the Rice Village, downtown, Richmond Strip, and the Montrose area. There are several good bars very close to campus, and dance clubs are closer to downtown. There is a really good live music scene here, as well."

Q "Well, you must be 21 to go places. Most people party on campus because it's so easy to drink. But the Village has some good bars, **downtown has more classy bars**, and the Marquis is a Rice student favorite—it's not a looker, but they have cheap Long Island Ice Teas."

Q "The parties are what you make of them. Often, there are a few college-hosted 'public' parties that can be a lot of fun, but often it's the smaller, private parties that have the most success. As a freshman, I attended every public party thrown, and I found that **some were bigger than others**. Now I know which ones are the big ones, and pretty much only bother going to those. Otherwise, they get really old really fast."

Q "On-campus parties generally consist of people getting drunk, and then **kind of halfway pretending to dance**. I'm personally not a big fan of them, but they seem to be pretty popular."

Q "Parties on campus are decent. They're better when you're an underclassman—upperclassmen get pretty tired of them and put in less of a showing. **We have a wet campus to prevent people going off campus to drink** at bars and clubs and getting into accidents driving back to campus. It also helps foster a safe drinking environment and teach students how to drink moderately and responsibly. So people rarely go off campus to bars and clubs. However, there are some great bars nearby in the Village, and there are some good clubs downtown."

Q "**Public and private parties are frequent and plentiful on campus**. Rice students tend to work hard and play hard, as a rule. Rice has the only officially 'wet campus' in Texas, which results in a much safer environment because students do not have to drive back from off-campus parties. However, if a different atmosphere is desired, there are plenty of good bars nearby, like The Volcano, Timberwolf, and several establishments in the Rice Village, located a mere two blocks from campus. There is also Willy's Pub on campus, which is the place to be on Thursday nights."

Q "Well, I hardly ever go off campus to party. However, I know that many people do go clubbing or bar hopping, so there are some out there. After all, **this is one of the largest cities in the United States**."

Q "Some **students take advantage of the Houston club scene**, and there are some underage clubs. I haven't been clubbing in Houston. If you are under 21, you can't get into any bars that I know of other than Willy's Pub in the student center. Pub night is every Thursday night, and it's a good time for students across campus to meet up and chill."

Q "Other than going to a few clubs as a freshman, I found that I didn't venture out into Houston often until I turned 21. During senior year, a lot of my friends were into going out to explore bars and pubs, and there are some really cozy, exciting, and different ones in Houston if you do your research. **A lot of the residential colleges host a Pub Crawl night**, when they rent a big bus and take anyone over 21 to four or five bars over a four-hour period. It was nice because we didn't have to worry about a designated driver, and we got to see some new places we'd never been to."

Q "**If you like R&B or rap, there will be plenty of clubs for you** (Club Spy, Shock, and more). As for techno, the Roxy hosts a decent night on Saturday. If you like 'real' techno, then Hyperia is an excellent after-hours club. If you're more into industrial/gothic/punk, then you're totally out of luck. Houston is definitely not San Francisco. For the most part, Houston residents are pretty straight-laced. There are plenty of bars around Houston, and I'd say they're pretty much like bars everywhere else."

Q "The parties on campus are frequent and the experience depends mostly on your mood. If you're looking for a fun, silly, drunk time and want to dance and ogle people in ridiculous outfits, college parties are great. They can get very rowdy, but there are always people looking out for you, should things get out of hand. If you've outgrown the on-campus party thing, or it was never really your style, there are some nice places to go out to around town. **The Timberwolf has almost every beer in existence on tap**, and it's a good place to go with a small group to chat and play shuffleboard. The Marquis is plenty shady, but can be a good time, and their long island ice teas are served in 12 ounce glasses. The Rice Village area is lined with pubs and bars, none of which stand out, but all of which can be fun with a large group. They are all within walking distance from campus."

The College Prowler Take On...
Nightlife

The biggest perk of having a wet campus (i.e. alcohol allowed), is that in addition to the two pubs on campus, parties are frequent and well attended. Rice students like themed parties, especially with costumes, and they also like their beer and liquor, so expect to find all of these in abundance. Despite the great potential for creativity, Rice students tend to cling more to tradition when it comes to parties. Each college has a number of public parties that they traditionally host, which are more or less the same every year. Private parties (i.e. advertised only by word of mouth, less likely to be themed, more your idea of a regular college party with music, dancing, booze) are more spontaneous. The Alcohol Policy allows students that are under 21 to drink at private parties, as long as the alcohol stays behind closed doors. Students that are over 21 can take their open containers all around campus, and have even been known to take them to class on occasion.

Off-campus house parties are not unheard of, but they tend to be associated with groups that are more isolated from the mainstream social scene (i.e. athletic teams, music or architecture students, disgruntled upperclassmen). Club hopping is more popular with underclassmen, but by senior year, the off-campus bar scene is the preferred option.

The College Prowler® Grade on

Nightlife: A

A high grade in Nightlife indicates that there are many bars and clubs in the area that are easily accessible and affordable. Other determining factors include the number of options for the under-21 crowd and the prevalence of house parties.

Greek Life

The Lowdown On...
Greek Life

Number of Fraternities:
0

Number of Sororities:
0

Rice has no Greek system. However, most students believe that the residential college system is much better!

Students Speak Out On...
Greek Life

{ **"The residential college system basically works like randomly-assigned, non-exclusive, inexpensive, coed Greek organizations."**

Q "There is no such thing as 'Greek life' on campus at Rice. **The colleges are kind of like fraternities/sororities** in that they give everyone a group to belong to, and they compete against each other."

Q "**We have residential colleges, and that's the best part of Rice**. It's much more like a family, and you stay in that same college for all your years at Rice."

Q "There are no frats or sororities at Rice. They are outlawed in the constitution. **The dorms are structured to be extremely close-knit**. Each dorm is almost like a coed frat house; everyone knows everyone."

Q "**There is none**! Whoopee!"

Q "**No Greek life at Rice, just dorms which basically serve as fraternities**. Each college has its own personality, traditions, and cheers. I personally find it a little juvenile, but every once and a while I get in the spirit. I lived off campus and loved it. I'll be on campus my senior year for convenience's sake. I'd say the downfall is that being in the same dorm for four years limits people from getting to know other people, but most people at Rice would want to burn me at the stake for saying such things. They love their colleges. More power to them."

Q "Instead of having a Greek system, Rice operates by something called the college system, modeled after one used by Oxford and other prestigious universities in England. Every incoming student is randomly assigned to one of nine residential colleges, each with their own traditions and camaraderie. The result is something like a smaller and more personable subset of the University; one that feels less like a dorm and more like a family. The strong bonding that takes place within the colleges, combined with the absolute all-inclusiveness, creates an **environment that possesses all the good elements of a Greek system and none of the bad**. Every college has its various strengths, points of pride, and odd quirks, but every Rice student is thoroughly convinced that his or her college is the best."

Q "We have something better than a Greek system. The whole school can be an active part of it if they choose to. It doesn't single people out the way Greek life does. College systems dominate the social scene in the way that the same people are at all the parties—these are the people you'll get to know if you choose to participate. Honestly, the college system is the most unique thing about Rice, and I think **it's a really nice aspect of campus life**."

The College Prowler Take On...
Greek Life

Rice students love the fact that Rice has no Greek life. It is nearly unanimous amongst students that the residential college system is far superior to the Greek system because it offers many of the positive aspects of the Greek system while eliminating the negative. The college system provides you with a small, tight-knit group of people from the time you enter Rice as a freshman. These people become a support network and a family. The colleges help you make friends and contacts with whom you share a common ground. The residential colleges also sponsor social, athletic, and cultural events. However, because of the random assignment, there is no degrading or stressful selection process to go through, and each college is home to individuals of all backgrounds, personality types, styles, strengths, and interests.

While most students feel very positive about the College System, many even naming it as one of the top reasons they chose to come to Rice, some students also point out that the system can limit students in their social life. This is a personal choice however, and there are plenty of ways to meet other students: classes, clubs and extracurricular organizations, plays, and athletic teams, to name a few. By the end of your first or second year, your residential college may begin to feel a bit confining: knowing everyone, knowing everyone's business, and knowing that they also know your business.

The College Prowler® Grade on

Greek Life: N/A

A high grade in Greek Life indicates that sororities and fraternities are not only present, but also active on campus. Other determining factors include the variety of houses available and the respect the Greek community receives from the rest of the campus.

Drug Scene

The Lowdown On...
Drug Scene

Most Prevalent Drugs on Campus:

Alcohol

Marijuana

Liquor-Related Referrals:

10

Liquor-Related Arrests:

0

Drug-Related Referrals:

8

Drug-Related Arrests:

1

Drug Counseling Programs

Confidential counseling, treatment, and rehabilitation programs are available to both students and employees. Students can contact the Rice Counseling Center at (713) 348-4867, the Rice Student Health Service at (713) 348-4966, or the Rice University Wellness Center at (713) 348-5194. All of these offices are located on campus.

Students Speak Out On...
Drug Scene

"For a college campus, I think the drug scene at Rice is very calm."

Q "Seek and ye shall find. Otherwise, drugs are easy to ignore. **There is usually enough alcohol to keep everyone happy**. But drugs are there if you look."

Q "I never ran into drugs. It's not something there's a lot of or any peer pressure about—I knew some people who did a lot of drugs, some with whom I was very close, and I never felt interested or bothered by it. **In terms of the alcohol scene, there's a lot of it**, and it's easy to find. Just make sure you know your limits, and you decide how much you want to be a part of the drinking scene before you start experimenting."

Q "I don't really know much about the drug scene. I knew a few people who used drugs, but **it was never something that was very prevalent** or that you'd really expect to come across."

Q "**There's pot, for the most part**. Anything worse is typically taken off campus; at least, you will never run into it if you don't hang out with people who do those things. Rice substitutes massive amounts of alcohol for drugs."

Q "I mean, it's there, but it depends on who you hang out with. **I have only heard of one kid getting kicked out for drug possession**."

Q "Drugs are accessible if you know the right people. But they're not overbearing. **If you're not into it, then you won't even realize it's there**."

Q "People drink a lot and use drugs sometimes. **It's really not a problem**. These are driven, motivated, and intelligent people."

Q "I don't know much about drugs on campus. **As far as I know, there isn't all that much**. Pot is available and around, but I don't think that the majority of the student population uses it. Alcohol is readily available since it's a wet campus. There are plenty of 21 year olds around, and pretty much everyone drinks. It's a major part of the social scene. The nice thing, though, is that there is never any pressure to drink or do drugs. Students recognize that it is a personal choice that one makes, and they respect that."

The College Prowler Take On...
Drug Scene

Most students feel that drugs are a non-issue at Rice. People that want them can seek them out, but for the most part you will rarely encounter anything other than alcohol unless you go looking for it. At Rice parties, alcohol plays a very key role and it's highly visible, but drugs are not. Most students know of a few people who experiment with drugs, and the school newspaper will occasionally inform students of a drug bust that involved Rice students. However, these occurrences are incredibly rare.

As far as the scene itself goes, pot is definitely the most widely-used illegal substance—most people who do experiment with drugs do so carefully, and one student mentioned that he'd only heard of one expulsion over drugs. All in all, the drug scene here is practically invisible. As with anywhere, it can be sought out, but it is certainly not prevalent and unavoidable.

The College Prowler® Grade on

Drug Scene: B+

A high grade in the Drug Scene indicates that drugs are not a noticeable part of campus life; drug use is not visible, and no pressure to use them seems to exist.

Campus Strictness

The Lowdown On...
Campus Strictness

What Are You Most Likely to Get Caught Doing on Campus?

- Parking illegally
- Drinking underage (if not following the Alcohol Policy)
- Drugs
- Cheating on homework/exams
- Illegal Cable
- Running through the Baker Fountain
- Steam Tunneling
- Pranks ("Jacks") on other residential colleges

Students Speak Out On...
Campus Strictness

"They're not strict at all, really. Since alcohol is allowed on campus, no one gets in much trouble for it. Underage drinkers are supposed to drink at 'private parties,' though."

"I don't think drug use (that people know about anyway) is tolerated, but drinking is another story. The alcohol policy is brilliant because they realize that college students drink, but by allowing the closed-door privacy policy, things are kept on campus so that safety is at a premium. **The Rice police officers are amazing, and they really are here to help students**."

"The campus police take a relaxed attitude towards drinking. If they don't see it, and it's not disturbing or harming anyone, then there's no problem. If someone is causing problems, they usually try to take care of it via on-campus means like **U-court or some other disciplinary action** instead of arresting people, unless the problem is extreme."

"I can't speak about drugs, but **in terms of drinking, they are not at all strict**—as long as you stay out of their way and don't hurt yourself or anyone else, nothing bad will happen to you. If you do get hurt, the campus police will usually take care of you without any punitive action being taken, even if you're underage."

Q "The police here aren't very strict when it comes to alcohol, but they do crack down on drugs. They don't try to get students in trouble, but if they think you're doing something illegal, they will call you on it. Alcohol is handled pretty leniently, though, and unless you're underage and completely intoxicated and making a racket, **they won't take you in**. They want to make sure you're safe, so they're much more likely to slap you with a warning and then help you home."

Q "The campus police are primarily concerned with the safety of the students, and they are definitely not out to nail anyone for alcohol violations as long as they are being relatively sensible and safe. Proper identification is required to be served alcohol at any public event, but as long as private events remain in control and do not bother anyone else, **there won't be any problems**. Drugs are a different matter, and students who are caught with any illegal substance should not expect similar leniency."

Q "**RUPD is strict with drug usage and consequences are very serious**. The alcohol policy that the campus follows is quite lax and formed more for the safety of the individual students. If, however, a student chooses to leave the campus, the Houston Police department will employ a far stricter and harsher degree of punishment."

Q "Campos are really lenient with drinking. They know underage drinking happens, but they figure if it stays on campus and if you're not driving, you're safe. People look out for each other, so drinking is not a big problem. I'm sure stuff happens that I don't hear about, but it's nothing really bad. **Drugs probably aren't a good idea to get caught with**. It probably happens in small amounts, but if it can be smelled by people walking around, you'll get busted."

Q "The alcohol policy at Rice is really laid-back. **You can have parties in your room as long as you register your keg in advance**, keep the door closed, and do not allow alcohol to leave the room. The campus police generally leave you alone, unless you are vomiting or urinating on something. It's hard to get in trouble for alcohol unless you try."

Q "One of the other wonderful things about the campus police is that they are very non-invasive. **They are not out to get students**—their job is to make sure that we stay healthy and safe. They want to promote responsibility, rather than bust students when they make the first stupid mistake of their lives. The Campos are great to work with, and great to be around, and we're lucky to have people who care as much as they do work with us every day to keep us safe, and at the same time, not interfere with the relaxed nature of the culture at Rice."

The College Prowler Take On...
Campus Strictness

For the most part, Rice students are very pleased with the relationship between the campus police and the student body. The prevailing attitude is that Campos are there for student protection and well-being. Students admit that the RUPD has no tolerance for drug-abuse. However, drug usage is not a large problem at Rice, and most students believe that drug offenders deserve whatever they get. The same attitude is taken for cheating on graded work or exams. Students tend to agree with the enforcement of the Honor Code and any disciplinary actions taken against cheaters.

The Rice alcohol policy allows students to drink on campus, including underage students, as long as they keep it behind closed doors in the atmosphere of a "private party." Because students recognize the alcohol policy as a privilege that can be lost if not handled responsibly, they usually take care of each other and monitor their friends' intake. The police care first about the safety of the students, and they are not out looking to bust underage drinkers. In fact, the only chance an underage drinker has of getting in trouble at Rice is if they blatantly violate the alcohol policy (i.e. drinking at a public party or at Pub), and they proceed to call attention to themselves or behave belligerently.

A-

The College Prowler® Grade on
Campus
Strictness: A-

A high Campus Strictness grade implies an overall lenient atmosphere; police and RAs are fairly tolerant, and the administration's rules are flexible.

Parking

The Lowdown On...
Parking

Parking Permit Cost:
Freshman $275
Upperclassmen $125

Rice Parking Services:
(713) 348-PARK (7275)
cormier@rice.edu
http://rupd.rice.edu/cars.html

**Freshman Allowed
to Park?**
Yes

**Common
Parking Tickets:**
No Parking Zone, Illegally
Parked Overtime: $25

Handicapped Zone: $50

Fire Lane: $50

Vehicle Booted (Lock placed
on your wheel after a number
of tickets): $75

Student Parking Lot?
Yes

→

Parking Permits

It is not at all difficult to obtain a parking permit as an undergraduate. Any student can get a permit to park in the stadium lot, and lucky upperclassmen (almost exclusively seniors and/or officers in student government) might get permits to park in the college lots, which are located much closer to the residential buildings.

Create-a-Parking-Spot

Rice has a great policy of 15-minute parking along the Inner loop and President's Drive (areas where parking is not permitted). Students can park their cars alongside the curb and leave their emergency lights blinking while they run into a building for an errand, drop something off for a friend, unload boxes, or whatever. While students do occasionally luck out and are able to leave their car parked in this manner for longer than 15 minutes, the campus police have really begun to step up their parking surveillance. If you don't want a ticket, you probably shouldn't risk it!

Did You Know?

Best Places to Find a Parking Spot

You can always find a spot in the Stadium Lot, and for upperclassmen with permits for the college lots, finding a spot is almost never a problem.

Good Luck Getting a Parking Spot Here!

At night and on the weekends, faculty lots open up to underclassmen. These usually don't fill up on weeknights, but you may have problems finding a spot on a Friday or Saturday night.

Students Speak Out On...
Parking

{ **"The parking scene is probably unparalleled. Parking is easy and moderately priced."**

Q "It is extremely easy to park on campus. I'm from New England, where parking lots are as valuable as gold, so I see the situation at Rice as a really great one. **It's not that expensive in comparison to other schools, and freshmen can have cars**."

Q "There is always a place to park, but it can be difficult to get a spot near where you are trying to go. **Residential college lots require a special sticker, which can be hard to get**, but parking is always available in the stadium, and there are shuttles that can take you all around campus."

Q "**Parking sucks**. They make you park at the stadium, which is a 10-15 minute walk from most residential colleges. Also, the parking gate system is a hassle and parking permits are pretty expensive considering that the parking is far away and uncovered."

Q "Parking is easy. **There are shuttles** that go from the parking lot to the colleges and vice-versa. You will always find parking."

Q "There is plenty of parking, but it is far away from where you will live—a half a mile or so. **We can move the cars right next to the dorms on weekends**. It is a complicated system, but it works well."

Q "**Parking is getting harder and harder, but it's better than at a lot of schools** with campuses that aren't as enclosed. You might have to pay a lot for parking, but there will be somewhere for you to keep your car that is no more than a 15-minute walk from where you live. However, this walk will seem a lot longer if some of your friends manage to get a spot right outside your dorm."

Q "Parking is great because of the fact that it exists—at other schools you have a heck of a time finding anywhere to park. Rice students tend to complain about parking because it is in the stadium, but **there is a shuttle that goes around, and it is only a 10-15 minute walk**, which is nothing."

Q "**To be honest, we hate the new parking system**. It's unnecessarily expensive, and the parking gates are a huge hassle. There isn't even a lack of parking spots out at the stadium, so it makes no sense to start charging students so much money. Plus, it makes it a lot more difficult for visitors to come and park at Rice. They have to go through this complicated process with the police station, and they are only allowed to park in certain areas of the stadium lot or pay money to park in the central parking garage underneath the new Jones Graduate School of Management."

The College Prowler Take On...
Parking

Students give mixed reviews on parking. Some students acknowledge that our parking situation is far superior to many schools. It is not a problem to get a spot. You just register your car, pay your fee, put the sticker on your window, and you are guaranteed a parking place in the stadium lot. To a transfer student or anyone from New England or most big cities, it sounds fabulous. The problem is that the parking system at Rice has been getting less convenient and more expensive with each passing year. A few short years ago, parking was free for all students. Then, with construction projects and the addition of new buildings and colleges, several lots shrunk or completely disappeared.

Parking is far away by Rice campus standards, especially if you are assigned to one of the North Colleges (10 to 12 minutes on foot). This isn't insurmountable, of course, but it does discourage spur of the moment late night trips to grab food or go visit your off-campus friends. Luckily, by the time you are a senior you have a pretty good shot at getting a parking place in one of the small college lots. These spots cost a bit more but are well worth the extra cash for the increased proximity and convenience.

The College Prowler® Grade on

Parking: B

A high grade in this section indicates that parking is both available and affordable, and that parking enforcement isn't overly severe.

Transportation

The Lowdown On...
Transportation

Ways to Get Around Town:

On Campus
Rice Campus Shuttle Service
Weekdays 6:30 a.m.-
10:40 p.m.

Rice Escort
Sunday 10 p.m–-6a.m.,
Monday–Thursday
10:30 p.m.–6:30 a.m., Friday
and Saturday night, by
request
(713) 348-6000

Taxi Cabs
Fiesta Cab (713) 236-9400
Liberty Cab (713) 695-6700
United Cab (713) 699-0000
Yellow Cab (713) 236-1111

Car Rentals

Advantage, national:
(800) 777-5500

Alamo, local: (713) 641-0533;
national: (800) GO ALAMO,
www.alamo.com

Avis, national: (800) 230-4898,
www.avis.com

Budget, national:
(800) 527-0700,
www.budget.com

Dollar, local: (866) 434-2226;
national: (800) 800-3665.
www.dollar.com

Enterprise, local:
(713) 645-7222, (281) 230-
8200; national: (800) 736-8222,
www.enterprise.com

Hertz, national: (800) 654-3131,
www.hertz.com

National, local: (713) 641-0533;
national: (800) 227-7368,
www.nationalcar.com

Best Ways to Get Around Town

Have a car. Have a car. Have
a car. Have a car. If you are
unfortunate enough to live in
Houston and NOT have a car,
you should make friends with
people who have cars. If you
MUST find alternate means
of transportation, try walking,
jogging, running, biking,
skating, taking the Metro bus,
a taxi, or the Light Rail.

Ways to Get Out of Town:

Airlines Serving Houston

American Airlines
(800) 433-7300,
http://www.aa.com

Continental (800) 433-7300,
www.continental.com

Delta, (800) 221-1212,
www.delta-air.com

Northwest (800) 225-2525,
http://www.nwa.com

Northwest, (800) 225-2525,
www.nwa.com

Southwest, (800) 435-9792,
www.southwest.com

TWA, (800) 221-2000,
www.twa.com

United, (800) 241-6522,
www.united.com

US Airways, (800) 428-4322,
www.usairways.com

Airports

George Bush Intercontinental
Airport (IAH), (281) 233-3000

IAH is about 24 miles and
approximately 40 minutes
driving time from Rice.

William P. Hobby International
Airport, (281) 233-3000

Hobby is about 12 miles and
approximately 20 minutes
driving time from Rice.

How to Get to the Airports

The Airport Express Shuttle travels between the Medical Center and both Houston airports at a rate of $15 per person (Hobby) or $20 per person (Intercontinental).

The shuttles run approximately hourly from both airports and deposit passengers directly in front of the Crowne Plaza, Holiday Inn and Suites, and Best Western hotels on Main St. The trip takes about an hour, depending on traffic, from Houston Intercontinental, and about 20 minutes from Hobby. To contact Airport Express, call (713) 523-8888.

A cab ride to the Hobby Airport costs $24-$28.

A cab ride to the Intercontinental Airport costs $42-46.

Greyhound

The Greyhound Bus Station is in Downtown Houston, approximately three miles from campus.

2121 Main Street

Houston TX 77002

(713) 759-6565 or
(713) 759-6581

http://www.greyhound.com

Amtrak

The Houston Amtrak station is located approximately five miles from campus.

902 Washington Avenue

Houston, TX 77002

1-800-USA-RAIL or
1-800-852-7245

*http://lb.amtrak.com/
stations/hos.html*

Did You Know?

The new president, David Leebron, recently initiated a program entitled "**Passport to Houston**." Its aim is to integrate the University with Houston's dynamic urban atmosphere, and, among other things, it provides students with free METRO passes, so they can hop on the new light rail system to get around town.

Travel Agents

A to Z Travels
3801 Kirby Dr. # 215
Houston, TX 77098
Main Phone: (713) 521-2150
Fax: (713) 521-3832

America Travel & Tours
6006 Bellaire Blvd. #101
Houston, TX 77081
(713) 666-4013

Hasti Travel
11814 Durrette Dr.
Houston, TX 77024
(713) 953-7353

International Tours
6363 Richmond Ave. # 200
Houston, TX 77057
(713) 785-2682

Travel Trends
1736 Sunset Blvd.
Houston, TX 77005
(713) 529-2500
Fax: (713) 529-2507

Voyager Travel
3930 Kirby Dr. # 203
Houston, TX 77098
(713) 524-7111
Fax: (713) 524-0499

Students Speak Out On...
Transportation

"It's hard to get off of campus. There are Houston bus stops around the outer loop, but the Houston bus system isn't that great."

"Public transportation in Houston is **slow and extremely inconvenient**."

"**Houston public transportation is awful**, although a light-rail stop was implemented right across the street from the main entrance to the University in 2004."

"Public transportation is unreliable and pretty shady. **Houston is a sprawling city and not much is within walking distance**, so a car (or a friend with a car) is a necessity for getting around in the city."

"Bring your car! Public transportation is non-existent— don't expect tons of buses and subways. And another thing—**the traffic here is crazy, and the distances are very long**."

"I ride the Metro, and it is fine. **You can get this thing called a U-Pass**, which allows students to ride the public bus for free."

"Besides a crappy bus system, Houston doesn't have any public transportation. Imagine **over four million commuters** trying to get out to the suburbs everyday."

Q "**There's a light rail system right outside Rice going to downtown**. I think they're trying to attract the Olympics here in 2012 or something, so that should probably grow. Buses are easy to get a hold of to go into downtown, but other than that, we usually just drive wherever. Either you or your roommates will probably have a car."

Q "There is a bus system, but I don't think it's a good idea to ride. They installed a light rail, too, but it's not yet fully operational. So for now, all that means is **lots of construction to drive through**."

Q "There really isn't any public transportation in Houston. The Metro (bus) is a bit scary and not exactly convenient to Rice, and I don't know anyone who's ever used it. The Metro Rail opened in 2004, and it takes students from the Med Center to downtown and around downtown. **Cars are still pretty necessary if one wants to go anywhere in Houston**, but the atmosphere of Rice lends itself to making that only a minor inconvenience. There's not usually a reason to leave campus, and there are enough people with cars that one can always find a ride."

The College Prowler Take On...
Transportation

Rice students all agree that public transportation in Houston is terribly inconvenient. While Amtrak, Greyhound, taxis, and the city Metro bus system are all available, Rice students rarely use any of these options. Metro bus stops are located very near to campus, but some students indicate that they do not feel safe riding the city buses, and the bus stops themselves are scary places if you are alone at night. The travel times on the city buses also vary with traffic, making them undependable, at best.

Most students have their own cars or rely on the kindness of their friends who have cars to get them around town. Houston traffic is a nightmare, as are Houston drivers (although students from other large US cities seem to think the driving is comparable). The recently completed Houston Light Rail has improved the public transportation situation slightly, although it has done little to alleviate traffic. The Rail has a Rice University stop and links the Rice campus to University of Houston downtown, two Houston Community College Campuses, the Houston Zoo, Market Square, Minute Maid Park, the new NFL stadium (Reliant), and some other popular destinations.

The College Prowler® Grade on

Transportation: D

A high grade for Transportation indicates that campus buses, public buses, cabs and rental cars are readily available and affordable. Other determining factors include proximity to an airport and the necessity of transportation.

Weather

The Lowdown On...
Weather

Average Temperature:

Fall: 72 °F
Winter: 56 °F
Spring: 70 °F
Summer: 84 °F

Average Precipitation:

Fall: 5.14 in.
Winter: 3.68 in.
Spring: 3.92 in.
Summer: 5.25 in.

Students Speak Out On...
Weather

"The weather is almost always hot and humid, so leave your sweaters at home. Even in the depth of winter, it rarely gets cold enough to require a jacket or long pants."

Q "Houston weather is kind of weird. Houston is considered a tropical climate. I think **the average rainfall is somewhere around 15 inches per year**. Anyway, at worst, it's hot and humid; at best, it's in the 70s and clear. It gets somewhat cold in the winter at times, maybe in the low 30s."

Q "If you're not used to the extreme humidity, then **it can be difficult to get used to**, and the air can be really oppressive at times. Most of the year, jeans, shorts, and T-shirts would be appropriate, plus some sweaters and light jackets for the winter."

Q "It will be beautiful for months, then rain for two weeks straight. This isn't like the rest of Texas—Houston is built on a swamp. So the rain stays in big puddles for weeks and **lets the mosquitoes breed**. In between rains, though, it's usually very nice. It's never too cold, and school ends early enough that it never gets that hot."

Q "**Weather is nasty**. Houston is hot and humid and gross. But it's something you deal with. You get used to not being able to fix your hair and constantly being covered in a layer of oil. Plus, the pollution is horrible."

Q "It doesn't get much worse than 40 degrees with rainy downpours, but by the same token, I was wearing shorts in January. When you first get to school it is hot and humid, but **everything is air conditioned**."

Q "The weather is as hot as they say, but it does get cold (even into the 30s) in the winter months, so **don't be fooled into leaving all your jackets at home**. Also, air-conditioning is rampant in the buildings, so bring plenty of light sweaters and wraps."

Q "The weather in Houston is usually mild, fairly hot, humid, and moist. Because of the city's proximity to the Gulf, there is a high humidity level most of the year. In summer, the city is very hot and humid, and thunderstorms are fairly common. **There is virtually no fall, and summer lasts up until around mid-October**. Winter is mild, often allowing one to run around in shorts up until Thanksgiving or later. Spring is usually a delight—although a bit wet as far as rain, it actually is nice out."

Q "The weather is not very nice at times. It can be really humid and hot and sticky and rainy. But during the winter, it cools off and dries out and is downright pleasant. Bring mostly summer clothes. However, classrooms and buildings tend to be cold because of the air-conditioning, so **have a few sweaters** and sweatshirts and light jeans, as well."

Q "I have got to complain about the weather. It is the only thing I hate about Houston—it is usually always humid and sticky! It never gets cold. It is usually warm and sunny, and it rains like crazy in August. So, **if you love the rain and you love being scantily clad**, then Houston is the place for you!"

The College Prowler Take On...
Weather

When you arrive for orientation week in August, be prepared to sweat like you have never sweated before. In the summer, Houston is unbearably hot and humid. Add to that the high pollution levels, and the result is frequent ozone warnings that caution against working or exercising outside during peak temperature hours. The mosquitoes come out in droves during these months, as well. Also be warned that when it rains, it pours. Think monsoon season. Several of the colleges have suffered flood damage in recent years, and a few upperclassmen tell very amusing tales about floating around the Inner Loop on inner tubes. After a particularly rainy spell, Rice campus will sometimes retain water for a long period of time, earning the affectionate nickname of William Rice's Marsh (a play on the name of our founder, William Marsh Rice).

The good news is that Houston has fairly mild winters, and extended fall and spring seasons. Long after your northern friends have dug out their sweaters and mittens, you can call home and brag to them that you went running outside in shorts and a tank top. You can enjoy outdoor picnics, pickup soccer games, or lazy reading in a hammock well into November. Once it cools off, and if it isn't raining, Houston weather is rather delightful. Don't be fooled however; it does get chilly, so bring a coat!

The College Prowler® Grade on

Weather: B-

A high Weather grade designates that temperatures are mild and rarely reach extremes, that the campus tends to be sunny rather than rainy, and that weather is fairly consistent rather than unpredictable.

RICE UNIVERSITY

Report Card Summary

A- ACADEMICS	**C+** GUYS
B+ LOCAL ATMOSPHERE	**C** GIRLS
A SAFETY & SECURITY	**B-** ATHLETICS
B+ COMPUTERS	**A** NIGHTLIFE
B FACILITIES	**N/A** GREEK LIFE
B- CAMPUS DINING	**B+** DRUG SCENE
A+ OFF-CAMPUS DINING	**A-** CAMPUS STRICTNESS
A CAMPUS HOUSING	**B** PARKING
A- OFF-CAMPUS HOUSING	**D** TRANSPORTATION
B DIVERSITY	**B-** WEATHER

Overall Experience

Students Speak Out On...
Overall Experience

"I love Rice! It's a small campus, so you don't feel lost all the time. You get to know the people you see every day. The college system is great, and the classes are all good."

"I've enjoyed my three years here. There's plenty of stuff to do and a diverse population here, so you'll find your right group of friends and something to get involved in. If you were the quiet type in high school, you'll be fine here. **If you like to party a lot, you'll be fine here**. I'm extremely happy here, and I honestly think anyone else can be, too."

Q "Overall, I had a good experience at Rice, but it took me the first two years to settle into my major and find the things that I like about Houston. **Don't get in a rut your freshman year**—try getting involved with a bunch of different groups of people, eating routines, and weekend hangouts. Then, figure out what feels comfortable and fun to you."

Q "Overall, I am highly pleased and completely satisfied with my college experience. I have no regrets and wouldn't trade it for anything. **I absolutely loved it, and it is hard for me to imagine a better place to go to school** than Rice. I wish I could go back and do it again."

Q "**I would say that I am happy at Rice about 95 percent of the time**. There is a lot of pressure at Rice to do well, but the students are not competitive with each other; they try to do their personal best. They tend to overwhelm themselves with lots of hard classes and activities and a social life, so when they get really busy, sleep suffers. But in general, I'd say that most Rice students are happy to be busy. I wanted to go to Rice to get away from my family and form my own identity. I succeeded in that respect, but sometimes I wish I was closer to home."

Q "I loved Rice. I just graduated in May, and I will miss being there next year, but for the most part, it's just the people I will miss. **The students make the school**. There are so many awesome, intelligent, talented, diverse students, and for the most part, everyone is extremely nice, friendly, and helpful. In such a small school, you'll get to know a large number of people really well. It's a great education and more affordable than many schools. After a few years, Houston will grow on you."

Q "I love my school. **Rice was my first choice, and it has lived up to everything I thought it would be and more**. I can't imagine going anywhere else, and things have worked out so well that I know that I will never regret the four wonderful years I'll have spent here."

Q "I love Rice. **It's got a wonderful atmosphere**, a gorgeous campus, excellent academics, and a constantly fascinating student body. I wouldn't want to be anywhere else. I don't know if Rice is the best place for everyone, but if you're serious about learning, not dependent on social cliques, and just a little bit quirky, it might be the perfect place for you."

Q "I like Rice because it is a very small school, and you realize that after a year; you see the same faces over and over again. It is very diverse, and if you are a party animal, there is plenty to do. If you are subtle and not into the party scene, you also have a great selection of things to do on campus. Overall, I began the year horribly. I hated it, and I wanted to go home. I adjusted to Rice and learned to appreciate where I found myself. **Since I am not a drinker, I had a problem dealing with the parties** and all the different activities that came with the alcohol. I learned to realize that it isn't as bad as it first seemed. You get used to it. I can honestly say I grew fond of the college I was placed in—supposedly the biggest party college on campus. You can imagine my horror at being placed at a college where I felt like I didn't fit in. But overall, I met great people, loved the professors and my classes, and learned a lot about the college life."

Q "I can't imagine **anywhere else in the world** that I'd rather be, and I really mean that."

Q "I liked Rice, but I'm glad to be out of there. I'll miss the classes and a few friends, but if I had it to do over again, I probably would have gone somewhere else. I know there are some people who loved Rice—it just probably wasn't the place for me. **It does have many great qualities** like the beautiful campus, wonderful professors, and interesting people."

Q "I'm a volunteer campus tour guide, and have been since second semester freshman year. **Every week, I show prospective students around our beautiful campus**, show them my room, and tell them about all the wonderful things Rice has to offer and the amazing things they could experience if they came here. I don't get paid to tell them the things I do, I volunteer my time because I love it here, and I want them to be as happy with their decision as I am. I hope that for some of them, Rice will be their choice, as well."

The College Prowler Take On...
Overall Experience

Overall, Rice students are highly satisfied with their college experiences. While they complain about some of the negative aspects of Houston (pollution, transportation, traffic, panhandlers), they also admit that there are many positive aspects to Rice's location (cultural and social opportunities of a big city, great restaurants!). Similarly, students have gripes about the University, including rising prices, the increasingly bleak parking situation, and a somewhat repetitive social scene (the same parties every year). Many aspects of Houston and Rice can be seen as both positive and negative. Houston weather is warm and temperate for the winter months, but it is oppressively hot and humid in the summer. Rice's small campus and student body are nice because they create a personal environment and allow students to meet more people and not just feel like faces in the crowd. However, students also claim that it begins to feel confining at times.

Rice students love the residential college system. They also find their coursework to be challenging, but manageable. With few exceptions, the instruction is very engaging, and professors are accessible and personally interested in students. Rice University is steeped in tradition, and some of these traditions (O-week, Willy Week, and Beer Bike) are the most anticipated social events of the year. Rice is small enough that these events bring together almost the entire student population. The traditions, high academic standards, and amazing people that make up the Rice community create an extraordinary and irreplaceable environment. While any Rice student would admit to the school's shortcomings, most believe the overall experience to be completely unique and unparalleled by any other university.

The Inside Scoop

The Lowdown On...
The Inside Scoop

Rice Slang

"Do you understand the words that are coming from my mouth?" Learn the lingo in advance, and you will wow your peers with your extensive, and ever-so-hip Rice vocabulary. (Thanks to the writers of the Jones College O-week booklet for their contributions!)

45-90-180 - Three big slabs of granite displayed in the engineering quad and tilted at these respective angles. Also known as "tipsy/sober/drunk." A good place to sun bathe, read, or go "star-gazing" with a "friend."

Academ - An arts, humanities, or social sciences major; opposite of an S.E.

All-nighter - What takes place after procrastination and before an extension.

Archi - Those unfortunate individuals who sell their souls to the architecture department and spend most of the college career in "studio."

Associate - A faculty, staff, or community member who is associated with a particular college, good people to get to know.

Backpage - Humor page of the *Thresher* (student paper) that serves as a forum for what the BP editors think is funny and enlightening to the rest of campus. See "Misclass."

Baker 13 - See Rice Traditions.

Bakerfeast - Rumored to be a party. See Rice Traditions.

Baker Fountain - Located near the Baker Institute, fun to run through, if you can avoid slipping or getting busted by the Campos.

Beer Bike - See Rice Traditions.

Beer-Golf - Usually a Friday afternoon or College Night activity involving golf clubs, beer, tennis balls, beer, the entire Rice campus as a course, and beer.

"Beyond the Hedges" - The world outside the hedges that surround the campus.

Big Three - Math 101, Chemistry 121, and Physics 101. The three classes that most S.E.s take their freshman year—known to convert a good number to Academs.

BPE - Backpage Editor

Bunny Grades - Service provided by the Registrar's office informing freshmen of their spring midterm grades and given out around Easter.

Campanile - The annual Rice yearbook, which you pay for with the blanket tax.
Also the name of the "bell tower" overlooking the Engineering Quad.

Campo - Campus Police

Care Package - Two words that parents don't seem to remember enough.

CENG (senj) - A chemical engineering major

Chem E - See CENG.

CIVI - Civil Engineering major

CK - Central Kitchen, replaced by new college serveries, but the food may always be known as CK.

College Night - Holiday typically sponsored once each semester at each of the residential colleges, usually involve themes to dress up or drink to.

Cougar High - University of Houston

Creamy J - Creamy Jalapeno, a specialty at Chuy's restaurant. You will find plenty of this at study breaks.

Dead Week - Not an entire week. The four days between the last day of classes and the first day of scheduled finals.

Diff-E - Short for "differential equations," one of the most lamented math courses at Rice.

EE (Double E) - Electrical engineering major. Remember kids, you can't spell geek without EE.

Esperanza - Fall formal sponsored by the Rice Program Council, a Sadie Hawkins-type dance in which the girls traditionally ask the guys.

Extension - Learn it, live it, love it. What you ask your prof for if you fall asleep in the middle of your all-nighter, or procrastinate just a little too much. SEs need not apply.

F&H - Food and Housing. See H&D.

Fairy Fountain - Fountain located between Jones College and Brown College. If you live at one of the North Colleges, and you have a birthday, you are going in.

Fondren - Rice Library.

Frog Wall - A wall on the entrance to the Archi building that makes frog noises if you run your fingers over the holes.

Gnome Cart (guh-no-me-cart) - Golf carts that F&H people use to get around campus. Favorite item to steal when drunk and/or stupid.

Graduate Student Association (GSA) - Just what it sounds like.

H&D - Housing and Dining. The new fancy name for F&H.

Hedges - Bushes that line the perimeter of the University and protect us from the outside world. Also found in the quad. See "hedge-jumping."

Hedge-jumping - A favorite past-time for daring or drunk underclassmen who attempt to hurdle (or at least fling their bodies) over the hedges in the quad.

Honor Code - What allows us to have take-home and unproctored exams/finals. The students take it seriously.

Honor Council - The protector/enforcer of the Honor Code, a student board responsible for investigations and trials of alleged Honor Code Violations.

Hook Up (v) - Can mean a variety of things, but usually refers to interpersonal relations from smooching to, well . . . you know.

House of Pies - Very popular all-night food-run spot.

Inner Loop - Somewhat circular road that passes through campus, approximately 1.4 miles around. Popular jogging path and the route of the Rice shuttles.

Ironman/Ironwoman - A person who chugs AND bikes at Beer Bike. (See Rice Traditions).

Jack - Pulling a prank on another college. Very popular during O-week and Beer Bike.

KTRU (kay troo) - Rice's student-run radio station.

Labbie - Fearless guides through lab-courses.

Ley Student Center - More likely to be called the RMC.

LPAP - Formerly known as "HPER," the Lifetime Physical Activity Program consists of a wide variety of P.E.-type classes. You will be required to take two before graduation.

Man, the - Any repressive force that attempts to squelch the spirit of Rice's student population.

Marquis II, the - Local "dive" bar, famous for its specials on Long Island Iced Teas.

MOB (Marching Owl Band) - The pride of halftime shows at Rice football games. Not your average Marching Band. Go check them out.

Masters - Faculty members who are chosen to reside with a college for five years and serve as surrogate parents. Get to know these guys; they are great connections and friends and will stand on your side if you should have a scrape with "The Man."

Matriculation - Opposite of graduation. Involves walking through the Sallyport into the quad as a symbolic act of being integrated into the University.

MSCI (Miskee) - Materials Science and Engineering

Meat Sheet - See Meet Sheet.

Mech E - Mechanical Engineering Student

Mecom Fountain - Located at the intersection of Main and Montrose. Expected birthday surprise for those turning 21.

Meet Sheet - Newcomers Guide published every fall containing pictures, names, colleges, and interests of incoming freshmen and transfer students. Freshmen are usually reduced to a row, column, and page number by upperclassmen.

Misclass - Part of the Backpage that takes humorous comments out of context. Contributions can be e-mailed to *backpage@rice.edu*.

Montrose - Artsy, bohemian area based around the intersection of Montrose and Westheimer. The center of the gay district in Houston.

Night of Decadence - See Rice Traditions.

OC - Off Campus

Orgo - Chem 211-212, Organic Chemistry

Outer Loop - Loop that circles around the outer edge of campus. Approx. three miles. Popular jogging path.

O-Week (Orientation week) - See Rice Traditions.

Owls - (In addition to being the mascot), Visiting high school seniors who have been accepted; Most come during Owl Weekend, an event sponsored by the admissions office in April.

PDR - Private Dining Room, located in the commons area of many residential colleges.

Pledge - "On my honor, I have neither given nor received any unauthorized aid on this homework/quiz/exam." Key component of the Honor Code, must be signed on almost anything you hand in at Rice. Might as well memorize it now.

Politico - Anyone who lives and dies to be elected, or at least to discuss policies and politics, not a compliment.

Prospective - High school students who come to Rice to check it out, also called a "Prospy."

The Pub - Willy's Pub, located in the basement of the RMC (Student Center).

Pub Rats - Regulars at Willy's Pub.

Pumpkin Grades - Service provided by the Registrar's office informing freshmen of their fall midterm grades, typically given out around Halloween.

Purity Test - Test containing 100 yes-or-no questions attesting to the relative "experience" of a person. Normally administered during O-week and at the end of senior year to see how much Rice has corrupted you.

The Quad - Area enclosed by Lovett, Rayzor, Sewall, and Anderson Halls, Fondren, and the Physics building.

Rally Club - Male exclusive club that meets before home football (and occasionally baseball or basketball) games. They wear white overalls, drink lots of beer, stumble to the games, and yell offensive cheers at opposing teams.

Rice Memorial Center (RMC) - The student center and home to the campus store, the Pub, Subway, the Rice Chapel, Sammy's, Smoothie King, and more.

Rondolet (Ron-duh-lay) - Annual Spring formal held around Beer Bike time, guys traditionally do the asking.

Room Draw (Jack) - Process in which rooms at each college are distributed. Freshmen are guaranteed housing and avoid the luck of the draw.

Rustication - Discipline option in which student is barred from attending campus events other than class.

SA (Student Association) - Governing body of the undergraduate students of the University, think student council.

Sally Club - Female equivalent of Rally Club

Sallyport - Big archway in the middle of Lovett Hall. See Rice Traditions.

Screw Your Roommate - See Rice Traditions.

SE - A science or engineering major

SMR - Student Maintenance Representative. Call this guy (or gal) if you want to rearrange your room, report unwelcome guests (i.e. ants, roaches, roommate's significant other), if something gets broken, or if you get locked out.

Steam Tunnel - System of underground tunnels connecting all the buildings at Rice. Exploring them is a "must do" before you graduate, but if you get caught, see "Rustication."

Study Break - A good thing to have after many long hours of slaving away on a paper or problem set. Usually involves food and drink. Can be university-wide, college-wide, or just a spontaneous trip to fast food with your friends. Also frequently sponsored by RAs, masters, or various clubs.

Taco Cabana (TC) - Favorite 24-hour Mexican joint known for tortillas and queso.

The Thresher - Rice student-run weekly newspaper.

The Trasher - The April Fool's newspaper, in no way affiliated with the *Thresher*.

University Blue - Rice's literary outlet for students. Filled with poetry, stories, photography, and artwork. Published in the spring and also known as *U-Blue*.

The Village - Shopping and dining area located close to Rice campus.

Virgin's Walk - Straight and narrow path that leads to the North Colleges. See Rice Traditions.

William Rice's Marsh - A play on the name of our founder to express what happens to campus whenever we have a good heavy Houston rain.

Willy Week - See Rice Traditions.

Willy's Statue - Located in the middle of the Quad. Willy's ashes are inside, making Rice the largest cemetery in the state of Texas.

Things I Wish I Knew Before Coming to Rice

On the Rice application, there is an empty box that applicants are supposed to "Fill with something that appeals to them." Don't put grains of rice in the box. I know, it sounds clever, but the Admissions office hates that.

Be careful not to get in over your head as a freshman. Be reasonable about your limitations. Rice kids were, for the most part, the overachievers of their high schools. However, it just won't work to start college, take a heavy course load, sign up for two intramural teams, run for a political office, and try out for your college musical. Start with a few things on your plate until you figure out how much you can stomach.

Then again, college is the time to explore. College is all about figuring out who you are. Shop around!!! Rice is a great place to step out of your comfort zone and try something you've never tried before: a new sport, your college musical, the improv comedy team, marching band, or writing for the newspaper. Also, do some exploring with your classes. Use your electives to try something new and interesting, or even shop around for your major. The perfect academic career that you have in mind when you start college might be very different from what you end up with!

Meet people outside of your college! The relationships you form within your college are awesome and will probably be the strongest you have at Rice. But you will start to feel really cramped after a year of two if you only hang out with people from your college. So cultivate other relationships, as well. Also, be warned that college gossip is awful. Dating, hookups, fighting; if it happens within your college, chances are good that everyone will soon know.

Tips to Succeed at Rice

Professors, RAs, and Masters are all on your side. Use them as connections; get to know them as friends. Make an effort to introduce yourself to your profs. Rice professors love that! And it will pay off later if you need an extension, hope for extra credit work, or want a letter of recommendation. Plus, it's amazing just to pick their brains. These people are brilliant in their areas of study, and they are excited to talk to you about your interests.

Don't be afraid. Rice can be an intimidating place at first. You won't be the "smart kid" that you always were in high school, because everyone here is exceptionally intelligent and hardworking. The cool thing is that once you are accepted, you can have full confidence that you belong here. For whatever reason, the Admissions Office decided that Rice needed a person like you, and they believed that you could handle the workload. So you should believe the same! Classes can be strenuous, but the work is manageable. You won't find the cut-throat competition at Rice that you find at other prestigious schools. So if you find that you need help, your fellow students are a great resource.

This is what your parents will tell you, but college goes by so fast! Live it up, and make the most of every opportunity!

Rice Urban Legends

One of the most classic and notorious Rice legends is simply the story of the mysterious demise of our founder, William Marsh Rice. Rice's valet, a man named Charles Jones, conspired with a crooked attorney, Albert Patrick, to kill Rice on September 23, 1900 and claim his fortune using a forged will. An autopsy, ordered by Rice's attorney, Captain James A. Baker (founder of Baker college), revealed evidence of poison. Jones testified against Patrick in order to receive immunity from prosecution, and in 1901, Patrick was convicted of murder and sent to Sing Sing. He was pardoned in 1912. Baker's actions allowed for Rice's actual will to be followed, and his estate left to the founding of Rice University. Rice's remains are buried under a large statue in the University Quad.

This leads nicely to another fabulous Rice legend, the story of a group of engineering students who, in 1988, decided that they were fed up with some recent decisions made by the administration. They concocted a plan to rotate the 2,000 pound statue of William Marsh Rice (located in the quad) 180 degrees, making Willy face Fondren Library for the first time in 58 years, thus turning his back on the Administration. The students elaborate plan was simulated on computers and tested off-campus on a 2,250 pound Toyota. According to legend, they removed the lights around the Quad two weeks prior to the prank, so that they could work in the dark without drawing attention. They also convinced campus police that the large A-frames used to rotate the statue were part of a school project, and were given a police escort to Entrance 8 when hauling the frames back onto campus after testing. The way the legend goes, the plan worked beautifully, except that one student, Patrick Dyson ('88) was caught. The University hired a group of real engineers to turn the statue to its rightful position, but these engineers somehow managed to damage the statue in the process (they claim the damage was done by the students). Dyson was given the responsibility of paying for the repair cost, as well as the cost of the engineering team. Students rallied behind Dyson. They printed and sold T-shirts that read, "Where There's A Willy, There's a Way " and actually made a profit after reimbursing the University. What took the Rice students one hour and $400 to do, took professionals three hours and a rumored $1,500- $2,000 to undo.

Rice pranks, or "jacks" are numerous. Some are clever while others are simply vile. One group of Brown College students once went out to eat at an all-you-can-eat Chinese buffet, and then snuck over to Baker College, where a Shakespeare production was underway. The students forced themselves to vomit all around the Commons and entrance areas to the building. Another prank, rumored to be motivated by the same Brown "mastermind," resulted in all the plumbing to Jones College being shut off for nearly a full day. In addition to preventing students from practicing good hygiene, the news of the prank did not travel fast enough to prevent several students from using the toilets, leaving an unpleasant smell to linger for the rest of the afternoon. For more historic Rice pranks, visit *http://staff.rice.edu/staff/Pranks.asp*.

Traditions

Baker 13
The proud Rice tradition of stripping naked, covering your body in shaving cream, running all around campus, and leaving body prints on various glass plate windows. Takes place on the 13th, 26th, and 31st of every month. If it is 10 p.m. on any of these days, and you catch the faint scent of shaving cream in the air, I'd recommend getting indoors very quickly. The runners will usually try to break into the residential colleges to leave prints on the inside, but are usually met by fierce (and often creative and borderline cruel) resistance. A few things to note: They will try to convince you to join them by chanting in zombie-fashion, "Join us!" The two unofficial rules of Baker 13 state that they can't touch you, and they must stop for all photo requests.

Bakerfeast
B-feast is "rumored to be a party," and you might not get much more information than that from anyone that has attended. This medieval themed event dates back to the days when Jones Residential College housed only females, and Baker College housed only males. The Baker lads invited the Jones ladies for a formal feast in their swank commons. Only Baker and Jones seniors (and lucky 21-year-old invited guests) are invited to attend this costume event. The only further information that to give you is that food and drink are free flowing, and the "rumor" is OH-so-true.

Beer Bike

By far the most hyped event on the Rice social calendar. More alumni return for Beer Bike than for Homecoming (at least, more young alumni). Undergrads begin prepping for this springtime event sometime in the fall. To break it into its simplest components: Beer Bike is a relay race of 10 bikers per team (men, women, and alumni) from each of the residential colleges, and the GSA. These bikers are joined by a team of 10 chuggers, who stand on a platform near the bike pit as each bike comes in, and must chug 24 (male) or 12 (women and alum) ounces of water or (yuck) warm and flat beer before the next biker can leave the pit. The hype leading up to the big day is huge (see "Willy Week" for more details). Most colleges (with the exception of Wiess) select a Beer Bike theme, print T-shirts, dye hair, paint faces, and more. They also fill water balloons—thousands and thousands of water balloons. These will be used for what will undoubtedly be the most wild, crazy, painful, and fun water balloon fight of your life. The Beer Bike parade that heads from Lovett Hall to the Bike track erupts in a colorful and wet exchange of ammunition between the colleges. Imagine it: almost every undergrad student at Rice participating in a cross-campus balloon fight. Oh yeah, it is *that* sweet.

Fountain tossing

Namely the Fairy Fountain and Meacom Fountain—this tradition is mainly popular with members of the North Colleges (Martel, Jones, and Brown) because of their closer proximity to the Fairy Fountain. If you should be lucky enough to have a birthday during the school year, your friends will know, you will be hunted down when you least expect it (or perhaps exactly when you expect it), and nabbed, carried, and tossed into the Fairy Fountain. The general idea is that you should run, fight, or resist, but not to the point of hurting anyone. Then, once they have tossed you in, you scramble to get up (carefully so that you don't slip!), all your friends bolt for the protection of the indoors, and you chase them down and try to repay them with big, wet hugs. Meacom (a public fountain about a block away) is basically the same idea, only this special honor is saved for your 21st birthday, and they may actually drive off and leave you to walk home.

NOD (Night of Decadence)

Cited by both *Playboy* and *Rolling Stone* as one of America's top 10 college parties, NOD has actually gotten a bit tamer over the last few years, due to the influence of a few concerned faculty members. Thrown by Wiess College every year around Halloween time, the party usually sponsors some witty play-on-words theme, such as: "Wizard of Nod," "Nod to Authority," "NeverNeverNod," "NODty or Nice," "2001, A Space Nodessy." The goal is basically to wear the least possible amount of clothing and still somehow fit with the theme. (Examples: tin funnel, strategically placed for "Wizard of Nod," Sheriff badges as pasties for "Nod to Authority"). Oh, and people tend to drink quite a bit. If you want an alternative activity for the evening, a lot of students choose to volunteer to work security, remain clothed, and look after their peers. (If you are lucky, they might let you use walkie-talkies or gnome carts!)

O-Week (Orientation Week)

The week before school starts in the fall, intended to welcome and acclimate Rice freshmen and transfers. While you will have to sit through a number of semi-boring (but important and useful!) discussions and meetings about policies, schedules, and more, O-week is really fun. You will be assigned to a random group of students from your residential college and to several upperclassmen advisors (a.k.a. mentors, fellows), who will be your guiding light in times of darkness or confusion. These advisors will help you sort out your classes, figure out that campus map, steer you away from bad professors or other bad choices, and generally explain the way things at Rice work. You will also get to experience exciting O-week activities within your college, like Scavenger Hunts (so much cooler than it sounds, I promise!), fun mixers, mock beer bike, skits, and broom ball. With your O-week group you might get the chance to: visit the Waterwall or House of Pies, late-night road-trip to Galveston, go Steam Tunneling, jump in the President's pool, and take the Purity Test. This is also when you will be brainwashed to believe that your residential college is far superior to the others. Don't expect a lot of sleep this week, but come with an open mind and get ready to meet amazing people and have a great time!

Sallyport

At Matriculation, during O-week of your freshman year, you will be marched through the Rice Sallyport, a large archway in Lovett Hall. You will walk from the opposite side of Lovett Hall into the Quad. You are greeted on the other side by a group of cheering advisors. This is symbolic of your entry into Rice. The tradition is that students cannot walk back out through the Sallyport again until the day of Graduation. After receiving your diploma, you walk from inside the Quad, through the Sallyport, to the opposite side of Lovett, where your cheering friends and family members will greet you. The story goes that if you should walk through the Sallyport again at all during your undergraduate career, you will be cursed and will never graduate from Rice. Even if you don't believe in such superstition, the walk out at Graduation is especially rewarding if you have actually waited the entire four years.

"Screw-Your-Roommate"

Annual Rice Program Council event in which people set up their roommates on a blind date and brainstorm creative ways for them to meet (a.k.a. find each other in the massive crowd that gathers on the quad). The Meet Sheet is an excellent resource to pick out potential dates. A few examples of set-ups: Woman dressed as Princess Jasmine; Man wheeled in on a cart, dressed as Aladdin, singing "A Whole New World." Man duck-taped to a tree; Woman sent to the Quad with an enormous pair of scissors. Woman dressed up in large cow costume; Man sent dressed as a farmer with a pail. At worst, the night is a bad date and a way to meet someone new; at best, people have actually found true love!

Virgin's Walk

The straight path that leads from the Inner Loop to the North Residential Colleges, so called because it was the path that led to the all-female dorms before the college system went coed. Myth has it that if you can knock out all of the lights along this path, you will get lucky that night (if you don't break all of your toes trying).

Willy Week

This is the week leading up to Beer Bike. Rice Program Council schedules events and TGs throughout the week, giving away T-shirts, and other Rice paraphernalia. Also, it's crunch time for Beer Bike preparations, and the most popular time to play Jacks on rival colleges. Students try to infiltrate other colleges, locate their stash of water balloons, and steal or destroy them. Many colleges have Willy Week vigilantes who stand guard, wearing camo, until all hours of the night to protect from balloon raids and other jacks.

School Spirit

School spirit may not look like it does at large state schools, but Rice students are very proud to attend Rice. We know that our University is amazing in many ways, and we value the education we are receiving in addition to the many "pluses" that are lacking at other prestigious universities (better price, incredible faculty, residential college system, honor code, take-home and non-proctored exams, alcohol policy and wet campus, and our many unique traditions). Class rings are very popular among Rice students. Alumni purchase rings to remember their time at Rice, as well as to recognize fellow alum who have shared the experience. Students may not have huge amounts of school spirit when it comes to going out and supporting our athletic teams (football and baseball aside), but your average Rice student would surely stand tall and give a dignified retort if anyone tried to put Rice down. There is almost a fierce pride and camaraderie amongst Rice students. We identify with each other, and we are proud of our school. And we will cheer and wear the gear, if the situation calls for it.

Finding a Job or Internship

The Lowdown On...
Finding a Job or Internship

If you are worried about finding a job or internship during your college career or after you graduate, take heart! Rice has a fabulous Career Services staff that is very capable and eager to help. Your connections with Rice faculty and other Rice students may also prove very advantageous in your search. Networking and building good relationships with your professors will definitely help you in the long run.

Advice

Don't feel like you have to have an internship every summer. Many students feel this kind of pressure, but remember that you have the rest of your lives to work real jobs, and you are still young. Some Rice students use their summers to travel, to rest up from a hard year of work, or to experience a more "fun summer job" (summer camp counseling, white water rafting river guide, whatever).

However, it cannot be denied that padding the resume and making connections through internships will give you a big one-up on your competitors when it comes time for a real job search.

Also, make use of Career Services as soon as possible. They offer guidance for all stages of the process, including choosing a major, thinking about career choices, building a resume, interviewing, and salary negotiation.

Career Center Resources & Services

Rice University Career Services Center

MS-521, P.O. Box 1892

Houston, TX 77251-1892

(713) 348-4055

http://careers.rice.edu/studentsplash.cfm

Career fairs/ campus recruiting

Career counseling

Career testing

Personality and interest testing

Career and Life Assessment Program

Interview practice

Resume and cover letter critiques

Internship/experience

Career Resources Library

Alumni contact service

International work opportunities

The Summer Jobs Program

Business etiquette luncheons

Graduate student workshops

Average Salary Information

The following statistics have been provided by the Rice University Career Services Center and represent the average starting salaries of Rice graduates, by major. It should be noted that many Rice students graduate with more than one degree, and the salary information is listed under each degree that they receive.

Job Title	Salary	Job Title	Salary
Architecture	$26,700	Kinesiology	$66,000
Art and Art History	$48,700	Linguistics	$24,600
Asian Studies	$28,000	Managerial Studies	$49,000
Biology	$23,600	Math Economic Analysis	$40,000
Biochemistry	$35,800	Mechanical Engineering	$42,800
Chemical Engineering	$58,900	Music	$12,700
Civil Engineering	$46,000	Philosophy	$40,000
CAAM	$30,000	Policy Studies	$35,100
Computer Science	$55,300	Political Science	$41,000
Economics	$47,100	Psychology	$45,600
Electrical Engineering	$54,500	Religious Studies	$36,800
English	$32,100	Sociology	$31,100
Environmental Engineering	$60,000	Spanish	$31,300
French Studies	$27,300	Statistics	$33,800
History	$36,200		

Graduates who Enter the Job Market Within

Six Months: 57%

One Year: N/A

Firms that Frequently Hire Graduates

Accenture

Bain and Company

BP America

Ernst & Young

ExxonMobil

IBM

JP Morgan Chase

Motorola

Shell

Teach for America

National Instruments

Alumni

The Lowdown On...
Alumni

Web Site:
http://alumni.rice.edu

Office:
Office of Alumni Affairs
alumni@rice.edu
1-800-RICE-ALU
(713) 348-4057

Major Alumni Events:
Homecoming
Beer Bike
Alumni College
President's Lecture Series

Services Available:
Lifetime e-mail forwarding
Online directory
Alumni networking (in conjunction with career services)
Special alumni interest groups

Alumni Publications:
Sallyport Magazine
Owlmanac
@Rice (Online Publication)

Did You Know?

Famous Rice Alums:

Howard Hughes (Class of 1927) - Yes, the Howard Hughes!

Mary E. Johnston (Class of 1941) - Editor, *Fortune* magazine

Herb Allen (Class of 1945) - Inventor of the Screw-pull corkscrew

Charles Duncan (Class of 1947) - former president and chairman of Coca Cola

William Hobby (Class of 1953) - Lt. Governor of Texas

Robert Curl (Class of 1954) - Nobelist in chemistry and Rice professor

Robert Wilson (Class of 1957) - Nobelist in physics & head of physics research at Bell Labs

Lynn Elsenhans (Class of 1959) - CEO, Shell International

Larry McMurtry (Class of 1960) - Author of *Last Picture Show, Lonesome Dove*

Bill Broyles (Class of 1965) - founding editor of *Texas Monthly*, editor in chief of *Newsweek*, co-creator of *China Beach*, screenwriter of such films as *Apollo 13*

Ron Bozman (Class of 1969) - producer of such films as *Silence of the Lambs* and *Philadelphia*

Student Organizations

(This is only a brief sampling of the clubs and organizations offered; a full listing is available at *www.ruf.rice.edu/~stact/clubs.html*)

Aikido Club
Alternative Medicine Society (RAMS)
American Association of Petroleum Geologists (AAPG)
Amnesty International *http://www.ruf.rice.edu/~amnesty/*
Badminton Club *http://www.owlnet.rice.edu/~lding/club/index.html*
Catholic Student Association *http://www.ruf.rice.edu/~cathcen/*
Civil Engineering Chi Epsilon
Cricket Club *http://www.owlnet.rice.edu/%7Esmdutta/cricket/*
Dance Society of Flamenco Arts
Equestrian Club
George R. Brown Forensics Society *http://www.ruf.rice.edu/~forensic/*
Golf Club
Graduate Christian Fellowship *http://www.ruf.rice.edu/%7Elukec/*
Habitat for Humanity *http://www.ruf.rice.edu/~habitat/*
Hong Kong Student Association
Interfaith Dialogue Association *http://www.ruf.rice.edu/~ida/*
Iranian Society

Juggling Club *http://hc.hanszen.rice.edu/~alkahn/juggling/*
Karaoke and DDR (Dance Dance Revolution) Club
Karate Club *http://www.ruf.rice.edu/~karate/*
Libertarians College Libertarian's
Light Opera Society *http://www.ruf.rice.edu/~rlos/*
Melodious Voices of Praise (MVP)
Muslim Student Association *www.rice.edu/msa*
NAACP, Rice University Chapter *http://www.ruf.rice.edu/~naacp/index.shtml*
Rice Outreach Mentoring Program (ROMP)
Radio- KTRU 91.7 FM *http://noise.ktru.org/*
Reformed University Fellowship *http://www.riceruf.com/*
Slam Poetry at Rice (SPAR) Club
Society of Petroleum Engineers *http://www.ruf.rice.edu/~spe/*
Society of Women Engineers (SWE) *http://www.ruf.rice.edu/~swe/*
Turkish Student Association (RTSA) *http://www.ruf.rice.edu/~rtsa/*
Ultimate Frisbee, Men's (Cloud Nine) *http://www.ruf.rice.edu/~ultimate/*
Wine Society
Yearbook- Campanile *www.ruf.rice.edu/~yearbook/*
Yoga Club *http://www.ece.rice.edu/~shri/yoga/*

The Best & Worst

The Ten BEST Things About Rice

1	The residential college system
2	Tremendous faculty and challenging academics
3	The alcohol policy/wet campus
4	The honor code
5	Willy Week/Beer Bike
6	Freshman orientation week
7	Amazingly brilliant, diverse, fun and interesting peers
8	The chance to explore a variety of Rice extracurriculars
9	Beautiful, small, safe campus; big city setting and cultural opportunities
10	Undergrad focus and opportunities (study abroad, research facilities)

The Ten **WORST** Things About Rice

1. Houston weather (can also be a good thing)

2. Houston pollution

3. Parking and public transportation

4. Increase in parking tickets

5. The residential college system can limit students' social circles

6. Small campus and student population begins to feel confining

7. Everyone is an overachiever, so people are often busy and stressed

8. Prices are going up—tuition meal-plans, and parking

9. On-campus social life can get repetitive and monotonous

10. Some profs focus more on research than teaching

Visiting

The Lowdown On...
Visiting

Hotel Information:

**Best Western Inn—
Greenway Plaza**

http://www.bestwestern.com/

2929 Southwest Fwy.

(713) 528-6161 or
(800) 937-8376

Fax: (713) 528-2985

Distance from Campus:
4 miles

Price Range: $79–$100
Discounted rates offered for
Rice-affiliated visits

**Best Western
Park Place Suites**

1400 Old Spanish Trail

(713) 796-1000

Fax: (713) 796-8055

Distance from Campus:
2.5 miles

Price Range: $89–$129

➜

Crowne Plaza Medical Center

6701 S. Main St.

(713) 797-1110 or
1-800-227-6963

Fax: (713) 797-1034

Distance from Campus:
.5 miles

Price Range: $99
Discounted rates offered for
Rice-affiliated visits

Econolodge

7905 S. Main St.

(713) 667-8200

Fax: (713) 665-6679

Distance from Campus:
2.5 miles

Price Range: $45–$49

Four Points Houston Southwest

2828 Southwest Fwy.

(713) 942-2111

Fax: (713) 526-8709

Distance from Campus:
3.5 miles

Price Range: $99–$120

Hilton Plaza Houston

6633 Travis St.

(713) 313-4000 or
(800) 345-6565

Fax: (713) 313-4660

Distance from Campus:
1 miles

Price Range: $90–$270

Discounted rates offered for
Rice-affiliated visits

Holiday Inn Hotel and Suites—Medical Center

6800 Main St.

Phone: (713) 528-7744 or
(800) 465-4329

Fax: (713) 528-6983

Distance from Campus:
1 mile

Price Range: $130–$140
Discounted rates offered for
Rice-affiliated visits

Homestead Village

7979 Fannin St.

(713) 797-0000 or
1-888-782-3473

Fax: (713) 797-1907

Distance from Campus:
2.5 miles

Price Range: $55–$65

Houston Marriott Medical Center Hotel

6580 Fannin St.

Phone: (713) 796-0080 or
1-800-228-9290

Fax: (713) 770-8100

Distance from Campus:
1.5 miles

Price Range: $79–$109
Discounted rates offered for
Rice-affiliated visits

Midtown Terrace

4640 Main St.

(713) 523-3777

Fax: (713) 523-7501

Distance from Campus:
1.75 miles

Price Range: $63–$69

La Colombe D'Or Suites

3410 Montrose Blvd.

(713) 524-7999

Fax: (713) 524-8923

Distance from Campus:
1.5 miles

Price Range: $195–$275
Discounted rates offered for
Rice-affiliated visits

La Quinta Inn

4015 Southwest Fwy.

(713) 623-4750 or
1-800-531-5900

Fax: (713) 963-0599

Distance from Campus:
6 miles

Price Range: $69–$99

Marriott Medical Center

6580 Fannin St.

Phone: (713) 796-0080 or
1-800-228-9290

Fax: (713) 770-8100

Distance from Campus:
1 mile

Price Range: $69–$79
Discounted rates offered for
Rice-affiliated visits

The Patrician B&B Inn

1200 Southmore Blvd.

(713) 523-1114 or
1-800-553-5797

Fax: (713) 523-0790

www.texasbnb.com

Distance from Campus:
1 mile

Price Range: $95–$150
Discounted rates offered for
Rice-affiliated visits

Radisson Hotel

www.radisson.com/home.jsp

8686 Kirby Dr.

(713) 748-3221 or
(800) 333-3333

Fax: (713) 795-8492

Distance from Campus:
3 miles

Price Range: $89–$99

Discounted rates offered for
Rice-affiliated visits

The Renaissance
Houston Hotel

6 Greenway Plaza, East

(713) 629-1200 or
1-800-468-3571

Fax: (713) 629-4702

Distance from Campus:
3.5 miles

Price Range: $109–$159

Residence Inn by Marriott

7710 Main St.

(713) 351-1000 or
1-800-331-3131

Fax: (713) 660-8019

Distance from Campus:
3 miles

Price Range: $129–$189

Discounted rates offered for
Rice-affiliated visits

Robin's Nest B&B Inn

www.therobin.com

4104 Greeley

Phone: (713) 528-5821 or (800) 622-8343

Fax: (713) 521-2154

Distance from Campus: 1.5 miles

Price Range: $89–$150 Discounted rates offered for Rice-affiliated visits

Rodeway Inn

www.choicehotels.com

6712 Morningside Dr.

(713) 663-6200 or (800) 228-2000

Fax: (713) 667-1425

Distance from Campus: 1.5 miles

Price Range: $45–$100

Discounted rates offered for Rice-affiliated visits

The Surrey House Hotel

8330 S. Main St.

(713) 667-9261 or (800) 800-9261

Fax: (713) 667-2139

Distance from Campus: 2.38 miles

Price Range: $50–$57

Discounted rates offered for Rice-affiliated visits

Wellesley Inn & Suites

www.wellesleyinnandsuites. com/hotels/hfhs.shtml

1301 S. Braeswood Blvd.

(713) 794-0800 or (800) 444-8888

Fax: (713) 794-0925

Distance from Campus: 1.21 miles

Price Range: $69–$89 Discounted rates for Rice-affiliated visits

Wyndham Warwick Hotel

http://houston.citysearch.com/ profile/9841118

5701 S. Main St.

(713) 526-1991 or (800) 298-6199

Fax: 713-639-4545

Distance from Campus: .38 miles

Price Range: $129–$159

Discounted rates offered for Rice-affiliated visits

Take a Campus Virtual Tour

www.rice.edu/maps/tour.html

Campus Tours:

Student-led tours of the campus are offered year-round at 11 a.m. and 3 p.m., Monday through Friday. On most Saturday mornings from September 7, 2002 through May 3, information sessions are offered at 9:30 a.m., followed by a tour at 10:30 a.m. Admissions Office is closed during most major holidays, and you should call to ensure that the office will be open when you visit.

To Schedule a Group Information Session or Interview

Information sessions are available every weekday at 2 p.m., no appointment necessary. From April through December, an information session is also available at 10 a.m.

Personal interviews are not required, but high school seniors wishing to interview on campus should contact the Admissions Office, allowing two weeks notice for scheduling an interview. For more information regarding on-campus and off-campus interviews, call (800) 527-6957 or (713) 348-7423, or visit *http://futureowls.rice.edu/futureowls/Admission_Interviews1.asp*.

Overnight Visits

High school seniors interested in spending the night on campus can make arrangements to spend up to two nights with a student in one of the residential colleges. In the fall, overnight visits will be available from mid-September through late November. In the spring, overnight visits will be available from late January through mid-April. The Admissions Office requests two weeks notice for scheduling overnight visits.

Owl Weekend

If admitted to Rice University, you will be invited to attend Vision Weekend (for minority students) and/or Owl Weekend. You will have the opportunity to stay with current Rice students for two days and nights in a residential college, attend classes, meet professors, learn about Rice social life and extracurricular organizations, and acquaint yourself with all that Rice has to offer.

Directions to Campus

Driving from the North
- Take US 59 South and exit at Greenbriar.
- Turn left on Greenbriar and follow it to Rice Blvd.
- Turn left onto Rice Boulevard, and Rice campus entry gates will be on your right.

Driving from the South
- Take US 59 North and exit at Greenbriar.
- Turn right on Greenbriar and follow it to Rice Boulevard.
- Turn left onto Rice Boulevard, and Rice campus entry gates will be on your right.

Driving from the East
- Take I-10 West to US 59 South.
- Take US 59 South to the Greenbriar exit.
- Exit and take a left under the freeway onto Greenbriar.
- Take a left onto Rice Boulevard, and Rice campus entry gates will be on your right.

Driving from the West
- Take I-10 east to 610 South.
- Take 610 South to 59 North.
- Exit at Greenbriar and take the first right after exiting.
- Turn left onto Rice Boulevard and Rice campus entry gates will be on your right.

Words to Know

Academic Probation – A suspension imposed on a student if he or she fails to keep up with the school's minimum academic requirements. Those unable to improve their grades after receiving this warning can face dismissal.

Beer Pong / Beirut – A drinking game involving cups of beer arranged in a pyramid shape on each side of a table. The goal is to get a ping pong ball into one of the opponent's cups by throwing the ball or hitting it with a paddle. If the ball lands in a cup, the opponent is required to drink the beer.

Bid – An invitation from a fraternity or sorority to 'pledge' (join) that specific house.

Blue-Light Phone – Brightly-colored phone posts with a blue light bulb on top. These phones exist for security purposes and are located at various outside locations around most campuses. In an emergency, a student can pick up one of these phones (free of charge) to connect with campus police or a security escort.

Campus Police – Police who are specifically assigned to a given institution. Campus police are typically not regular city officers; they are employed by the university in a full-time capacity.

Club Sports – A level of sports that falls somewhere between varsity and intramural. If a student is unable to commit to a varsity team but has a lot of passion for athletics, a club sport could be a better, less intense option. Even less demanding, intramural (IM) sports often involve no traveling and considerably less time.

Cocaine – An illegal drug. Also known as "coke" or "blow," cocaine often resembles a white crystalline or powdery substance. It is highly addictive and dangerous.

Common Application – An application with which students can apply to multiple schools.

Course Registration – The period of official class selection for the upcoming quarter or semester. Prior to registration, it is best to prepare several back-up courses in case a particular class becomes full. If a course is full, students can place themselves on the waitlist, although this still does not guarantee entry.

Division Athletics – Athletic classifications range from Division I to Division III. Division IA is the most competitive, while Division III is considered to be the least competitive.

Dorm – A dorm (or dormitory) is an on-campus housing facility. Dorms can provide a range of options from suite-style rooms to more communal options that include shared bathrooms. Most first-year students live in dorms. Some upperclassmen who wish to stay on campus also choose this option.

Early Action – An application option with which a student can apply to a school and receive an early acceptance response without a binding commitment. This system is becoming less and less available.

Early Decision – An application option that students should use only if they are certain they plan to attend the school in question. If a student applies using the early decision option and is admitted, he or she is required and bound to attend that university. Admission rates are usually higher among students who apply through early decision, as the student is clearly indicating that the school is his or her first choice.

Ecstasy – An illegal drug. Also known as "E" or "X," ecstasy looks like a pill and most resembles an aspirin. Considered a party drug, ecstasy is very dangerous and can be deadly.

Ethernet – An extremely fast Internet connection available in most university-owned residence halls. To use an Ethernet connection properly, a student will need a network card and cable for his or her computer.

Fake ID – A counterfeit identification card that contains false information. Most commonly, students get fake IDs with altered birthdates so that they appear to be older than 21 (and therefore of legal drinking age). Even though it is illegal, many college students have fake IDs in hopes of purchasing alcohol or getting into bars.

Frosh – Slang for "freshman" or "freshmen."

Hazing – Initiation rituals administered by some fraternities or sororities as part of the pledging process. Many universities have outlawed hazing due to its degrading and sometimes dangerous nature.

Intramurals (IMs) – A popular, and usually free, sport league in which students create teams and compete against one another. These sports vary in competitiveness and can include a range of activities—everything from billiards to water polo. IM sports are a great way to meet people with similar interests.

Keg – Officially called a half-barrel, a keg contains roughly 200 12-ounce servings of beer.

LSD – An illegal drug. Also known as acid, this hallucinogenic drug most commonly resembles a tab of paper.

Marijuana – An illegal drug. Also known as weed or pot; along with alcohol, marijuana is one of the most commonly-found drugs on campuses across the country.

Major –The focal point of a student's college studies; a specific topic that is studied for a degree. Examples of majors include physics, English, history, computer science, economics, business, and music. Many students decide on a specific major before arriving on campus, while others are simply "undecided" until delcaring a major. Those who are extremely interested in two areas can also choose to double major.

Meal Block – The equivalent of one meal. Students on a meal plan usually receive a fixed number of meals per week. Each meal, or "block," can be redeemed at the school's dining facilities in place of cash. Often, a student's weekly allotment of meal blocks will be forfeited if not used.

Minor – An additional focal point in a student's education. Often serving as a complement or addition to a student's main area of focus, a minor has fewer requirements and prerequisites to fulfill than a major. Minors are not required for graduation from most schools; however some students who want to explore many different interests choose to pursue both a major and a minor.

Mushrooms – An illegal drug. Also known as "'shrooms," this drug resembles regular mushrooms but is extremely hallucinogenic.

Off-Campus Housing – Housing from a particular landlord or rental group that is not affiliated with the university. Depending on the college, off-campus housing can range from extremely popular to non-existent. Students who choose to live off campus are typically given more freedom, but they also have to deal with possible subletting scenarios, furniture, bills, and other issues. In addition to these factors, rental prices and distance often affect a student's decision to move off campus.

Office Hours – Time that teachers set aside for students who have questions about coursework. Office hours are a good forum for students to go over any problems and to show interest in the subject material.

Pledging – The early phase of joining a fraternity or sorority, pledging takes place after a student has gone through rush and received a bid. Pledging usually lasts between one and two semesters. Once the pledging period is complete and a particular student has done everything that is required to become a member, that student is considered a brother or sister. If a fraternity or a sorority would decide to "haze" a group of students, this initiation would take place during the pledging period.

Private Institution – A school that does not use tax revenue to subsidize education costs. Private schools typically cost more than public schools and are usually smaller.

Prof – Slang for "professor."

Public Institution – A school that uses tax revenue to subsidize education costs. Public schools are often a good value for in-state residents and tend to be larger than most private colleges.

Quarter System (or Trimester System) – A type of academic calendar system. In this setup, students take classes for three academic periods. The first quarter usually starts in late September or early October and concludes right before Christmas. The second quarter usually starts around early to mid–January and finishes up around March or April. The last academic quarter, or "third quarter," usually starts in late March or early April and finishes up in late May or Mid-June. The fourth quarter is summer. The major difference between the quarter system and semester system is that students take more, less comprehensive courses under the quarter calendar.

RA (Resident Assistant) – A student leader who is assigned to a particular floor in a dormitory in order to help to the other students who live there. An RA's duties include ensuring student safety and providing assistance wherever possible.

Recitation – An extension of a specific course; a review session. Some classes, particularly large lectures, are supplemented with mandatory recitation sessions that provide a relatively personal class setting.

Rolling Admissions – A form of admissions. Most commonly found at public institutions, schools with this type of policy continue to accept students throughout the year until their class sizes are met. For example, some schools begin accepting students as early as December and will continue to do so until April or May.

Room and Board – This figure is typically the combined cost of a university-owned room and a meal plan.

Room Draw/Housing Lottery – A common way to pick on-campus room assignments for the following year. If a student decides to remain in university-owned housing, he or she is assigned a unique number that, along with seniority, is used to determine his or her housing for the next year.

Rush – The period in which students can meet the brothers and sisters of a particular chapter and find out if a given fraternity or sorority is right for them. Rushing a fraternity or a sorority is not a requirement at any school. The goal of rush is to give students who are serious about pledging a feel for what to expect.

Semester System – The most common type of academic calendar system at college campuses. This setup typically includes two semesters in a given school year. The fall semester starts around the end of August or early September and concludes before winter vacation. The spring semester usually starts in mid-January and ends in late April or May.

Student Center/Rec Center/Student Union – A common area on campus that often contains study areas, recreation facilities, and eateries. This building is often a good place to meet up with fellow students; depending on the school, the student center can have a huge role or a non-existent role in campus life.

Student ID – A university-issued photo ID that serves as a student's key to school-related functions. Some schools require students to show these cards in order to get into dorms, libraries, cafeterias, and other facilities. In addition to storing meal plan information, in some cases, a student ID can actually work as a debit card and allow students to purchase things from bookstores or local shops.

Suite – A type of dorm room. Unlike dorms that feature communal bathrooms shared by the entire floor, suites offer bathrooms shared only among the suite. Suite-style dorm rooms can house anywhere from two to ten students.

TA (Teacher's Assistant) – An undergraduate or grad student who helps in some manner with a specific course. In some cases, a TA will teach a class, assist a professor, grade assignments, or conduct office hours.

Undergraduate – A student in the process of studying for his or her bachelor's degree.

ABOUT THE AUTHOR

Julia Schwent, a native of the tiny mid-western town of Festus, Missouri, spent her childhood years dabbling in writing, reading, make-believing, and attending summer camps. In high school, she unleashed her inner ham through speech and theater, made beautiful music through marching and concert band, helped to run a few honors and service clubs and organizations, and stayed busily involved in general until graduating valedictorian from Herculaneum High School in 1999. She packed up her things and headed south to the Lone Star State in search of a higher education, a vocational calling, and a livelier social life than Festus had previously provided.

Julia spent the next four years at Rice University, thoroughly enjoying her higher education and newfound social life, while still managing to avoid any pesky vocational callings. In college, she continued to pursue her love of fine arts through photography, drawing, and theater (directing, producing, and starring in such shows as *Cat on a Hot Tin Roof*, *Nunsense*, *Pippin*, and *Company*). Unable to let go of her childhood, she returned to Missouri to reclaim her summer camp glory days, and spent four summers as a camp counselor, sporting a whistle, a campy nickname, and a vast repertoire of kiddie campfire songs.

In addition to writing this book, Julia currently works as a social research assistant for the National Center for Early Development and Learning. She hopes to work abroad in the upcoming year in order to further master the Spanish language, and afterwards plans to pursue graduate studies in the area of her vocational calling, if she should ever happen upon it.

Julia would like to thank her family and friends for their love, friendship, and unconditional support, and God for guiding her always. She would like to dedicate this book "To Dad, Mom, Laura, and Alex, the most important people in my life, through it all."

Feel free to contact Julia at JuliaSchwent@collegeprowler.com.

California Colleges

California dreamin'?
This book is a must have for you!

CALIFORNIA COLLEGES
7¼" X 10", 762 Pages Paperback
$29.95 Retail
1-59658-501-3

Stanford, UC Berkeley, Caltech—California is home
to some of America's greatest institutes of higher
learning. *California Colleges* gives the lowdown on 24
of the best, side by side, in one prodigious volume.

New England Colleges

Looking for peace in the Northeast?
Pick up this regional guide to New England!

NEW ENGLAND COLLEGES
7¼" X 10", 1015 Pages Paperback
$29.95 Retail
1-59658-504-8

New England is the birthplace of many prestigious
universities, and with so many to choose from, picking
the right school can be a tough decision. With inside
information on over 34 competive Northeastern
schools, *New England Colleges* provides the same
high-quality information prospective students expect
from College Prowler in one all-inclusive,
easy-to-use reference.

Schools of the South

Headin' down south? This book will help you find your way to the perfect school!

SCHOOLS OF THE SOUTH
7¼" X 10", 773 Pages Paperback
$29.95 Retail
1-59658-503-X

Southern pride is always strong. Whether it's across town or across state, many Southern students are devoted to their home sweet home. *Schools of the South* offers an honest student perspective on 36 universities available south of the Mason-Dixon.

Untangling
the Ivy League

The ultimate book for everything Ivy!

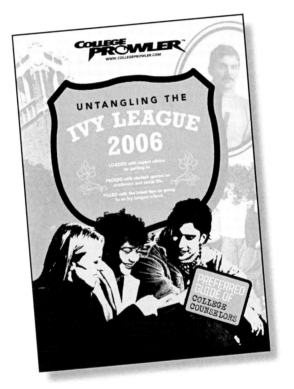

UNTANGLING THE IVY LEAGUE
7¼" X 10", 567 Pages Paperback
$24.95 Retail
1-59658-500-5

Ivy League students, alumni, admissions officers,
and other top insiders get together to tell it like it is.
Untangling the Ivy League covers every aspect—from
admissions and athletics to secret societies and urban
legends—of the nation's eight oldest, wealthiest, and
most competitive colleges and universities.

Need Help Paying For School?

Apply for our scholarship!

College Prowler awards thousands of dollars a year to students who compose the best essays. E-mail scholarship@collegeprowler.com for more information, or call 1-800-290-2682.

Apply now at ***www.collegeprowler.com***

Tell Us What Life Is Really Like at Your School!

Have you ever wanted to let people know what your college is really like? Now's your chance to help millions of high school students choose the right college.

Let your voice be heard.

Check out *www.collegeprowler.com* for more info!

Need More Help?

Do you have more questions about this school? Can't find a certain statistic? College Prowler is here to help. We are the best source of college information out there. We have a network of thousands of students who can get the latest information on any school to you ASAP. E-mail us at info@collegeprowler.com with your college-related questions.

E-Mail Us Your College-Related Questions!

Check out *www.collegeprowler.com* for more details.
1-800-290-2682

Albion College
Alfred University
Allegheny College
American University
Amherst College
Arizona State University
Auburn University
Babson College
Ball State University
Bard College
Barnard College
Bates College
Baylor University
Beloit College
Bentley College
Binghamton University
Birmingham Southern College
Boston College
Boston University
Bowdoin College
Brandeis University
Brigham Young University
Brown University
Bryn Mawr College
Bucknell University
Cal Poly
Cal Poly Pomona
Cal State Northridge
Cal State Sacramento
Caltech
Carleton College
Carnegie Mellon University
Case Western Reserve
Centenary College of Louisiana
Centre College
Claremont McKenna College
Clark Atlanta University
Clark University
Clemson University
Colby College
Colgate University
College of Charleston
College of the Holy Cross
College of William & Mary
College of Wooster
Colorado College
Columbia University
Connecticut College
Cornell University
Creighton University
CUNY Hunters College
Dartmouth College
Davidson College
Denison University
DePauw University
Dickinson College
Drexel University
Duke University
Duquesne University
Earlham College
East Carolina University
Elon University
Emerson College
Emory University
FIT
Florida State University
Fordham University

Franklin & Marshall College
Furman University
Geneva College
George Washington University
Georgetown University
Georgia Tech
Gettysburg College
Gonzaga University
Goucher College
Grinnell College
Grove City College
Guilford College
Gustavus Adolphus College
Hamilton College
Hampshire College
Hampton University
Hanover College
Harvard University
Harvey Mudd College
Haverford College
Hofstra University
Hollins University
Howard University
Idaho State University
Illinois State University
Illinois Wesleyan University
Indiana University
Iowa State University
Ithaca College
IUPUI
James Madison University
Johns Hopkins University
Juniata College
Kansas State
Kent State University
Kenyon College
Lafayette College
LaRoche College
Lawrence University
Lehigh University
Lewis & Clark College
Louisiana State University
Loyola College in Maryland
Loyola Marymount University
Loyola University Chicago
Loyola University New Orleans
Macalester College
Marlboro College
Marquette University
McGill University
Miami University of Ohio
Michigan State University
Middle Tennessee State
Middlebury College
Millsaps College
MIT
Montana State University
Mount Holyoke College
Muhlenberg College
New York University
North Carolina State
Northeastern University
Northern Arizona University
Northern Illinois University
Northwestern University
Oberlin College
Occidental College

Ohio State University
Ohio University
Ohio Wesleyan University
Old Dominion University
Penn State University
Pepperdine University
Pitzer College
Pomona College
Princeton University
Providence College
Purdue University
Reed College
Rensselaer Polytechnic Institute
Rhode Island School of Design
Rhodes College
Rice University
Rochester Institute of Technology
Rollins College
Rutgers University
San Diego State University
Santa Clara University
Sarah Lawrence College
Scripps College
Seattle University
Seton Hall University
Simmons College
Skidmore College
Slippery Rock
Smith College
Southern Methodist University
Southwestern University
Spelman College
St. Joseph's University Philadelphia
St. John's University
St. Louis University
St. Olaf College
Stanford University
Stetson University
Stony Brook University
Susquhanna University
Swarthmore College
Syracuse University
Temple University
Tennessee State University
Texas A & M University
Texas Christian University
Towson University
Trinity College Connecticut
Trinity University Texas
Truman State
Tufts University
Tulane University
UC Berkeley
UC Davis
UC Irvine
UC Riverside
UC San Diego
UC Santa Barbara
UC Santa Cruz
UCLA
Union College
University at Albany
University at Buffalo
University of Alabama
University of Arizona
University of Central Florida
University of Chicago

University of Colorado
University of Connecticut
University of Delaware
University of Denver
University of Florida
University of Georgia
University of Illinois
University of Iowa
University of Kansas
University of Kentucky
University of Maine
University of Maryland
University of Massachusetts
University of Miami
University of Michigan
University of Minnesota
University of Mississippi
University of Missouri
University of Nebraska
University of New Hampshire
University of North Carolina
University of Notre Dame
University of Oklahoma
University of Oregon
University of Pennsylvania
University of Pittsburgh
University of Puget Sound
University of Rhode Island
University of Richmond
University of Rochester
University of San Diego
University of San Francisco
University of South Carolina
University of South Dakota
University of South Florida
University of Southern California
University of Tennessee
University of Texas
University of Utah
University of Vermont
University of Virginia
University of Washington
University of Wisconsin
UNLV
Ursinus College
Valparaiso University
Vanderbilt University
Vassar College
Villanova University
Virginia Tech
Wake Forest University
Warren Wilson College
Washington and Lee University
Washington University in St. Louis
Wellesley College
Wesleyan University
West Point
West Virginia University
Wheaton College IL
Wheaton College MA
Whitman College
Wilkes University
Williams College
Xavier University
Yale University